CW01017704

A Key to the Drama

by And of the Theatre Gentleman No Professed Author but a Lover
of History

Address:
HardPress
8345 NW 66TH ST #2561
MIAMI FL 33166-2626
USA
Email: info@hardpress.net

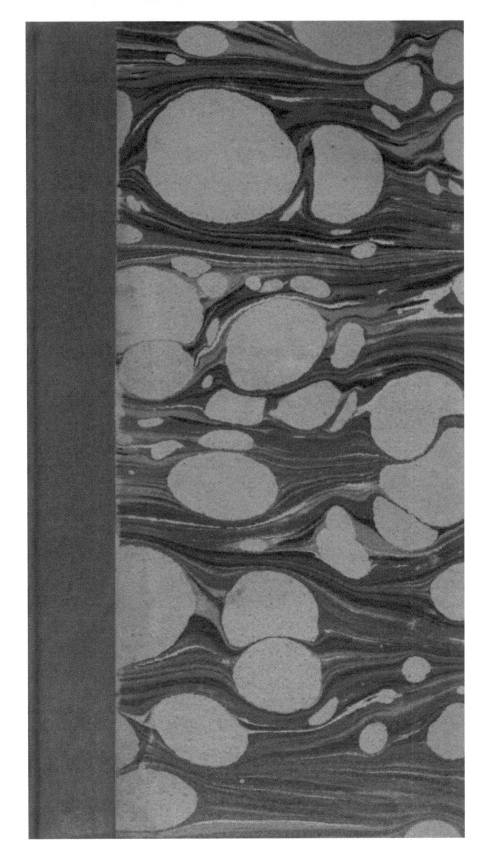

and Secret History

OF

MACBETH.

GENTLEMAN,

but a Lover of History, and of
the THEATRE.

N:

No. 71.

TO
HER GRACE
THE
Dutchefs of *Hamilton*, &c.

MADAM,

AT the fame time that the Author of the following Sheets is very far from thinking they have fufficient merit to introduce them to the countenance of the refpectable Name to whom they are humbly dedicated; and that his confined fituation ren-

dered

DEDICATION.

dered it impracticable for him to supplicate *Your Grace*'s permiffion; yet he flatters himfelf, that the confiderations which fuggefted *Your Grace* to him as the propereft Perfonage in *Great Britain* to prefent them to, may prevail with Your goodnefs to judge fomewhat favourably of his prefumption.

THE two moft illuftrious characters in the performance, are the anceftors of that *noble family*, whofe acknowledged eminence could only gain additional luftre by a connection with *Your Grace*.

WHILST the Author was penning the tranfcendent *virtues* and unequalled *beauty* of EUGENIA,

he

he could not help thinking of *the Dutchefs of Hamilton.*

WHEN he thought of the fair *Eugenia*'s having tranfmitted to pofterity a progeny, not lefs diftinguifhed for patriotic heroifm, than for every quality which renders mankind ufeful and amiable in fociety; moft natural was the reflection, That the celebrated *Dutchefs of Hamilton* had been chofen by Providence to perpetuate fuch a fucceffion.

IT was for thefe reafons, *Madam*, and for thefe reafons only, that he took the liberty to dignify the opening of his Work (a flight one as it is) with a Name fo illuftrious: for the accomplifh-

ments

DEDICATION.

ments which compleat *Your Grace*'s character, are so univerfally assented to, as equalled by few, exceeded by none; that he cannot even indulge a vanity of concluding it possible for him to be, with greater admiration and respect than every body else,

MADAM,

Your Grace's most obedient,

And most humble Servant,

The AUTHOR.

PRE-

PREFACE.

AS the representation or perufal of Plays, particularly thofe of the hiftorical kind, although a very rational entertainment, may in many cafes mifguide the judgment of an inattentive fpectator or reader, by fubftituting implicitly the matter in the play for the genuine hiftory of the times and perfons reprefented; our Author having beftowed a good deal of pains in examining into the fecret hiftories of the *Dramatis Perfonæ*, efpecially of thofe brought upon the ftage by the celebrated *Shakefpear*, thought he might employ his time worfe, than to communicate what materials he had collected from his examinations.

'He had begun, and was preparing for the prefs a particular Hiftory of *King Henry* VIII. when a friend made him an offer of the materials which compofe

compose this Volume, on condition
that he would give them the first place
in his Publication; and as the Tragedy
of *Macbeth* is one of those, of the same
inimitable Poet, which makes its appearance upon the stage, as often at
least, and with as much applause, as
any other, he chearfully agreed to the
proposal; and the rather, that few
memoirs furnish a series of more daring
enterprizes, affecting incidents, amazing intrigues, and profound plots, than
those which are to be met with in the
secret history before us.

WITH regard to facts, he has strictly
adhered to the materials; but as to the
language, that being almost obsolete,
he has endeavoured to modernize it.

IT may be necessary to premise to
censorious readers, that the modes of
thinking, acting, and writing, some
hundred years ago, (especially in the
northern parts of this island) not being
circumscribed by the same rules of de-
cent policy, by which they have been
since

ſince improved, it was impoſſible, without deviating from the originals, to maintain that inoffenſive chaſteneſs, with which the memoirs of later ages might be tranſmitted.

Bellona and *Venus*, how much ſo-ever diſtinct and incompatible are their excitements and operations, appear, in the days of King *Duncan* and *Macbeth*, to have been ruling planets : yet he has endeavoured, as much as in him lay, ſo to repreſent facts, that the mind, al-though it may be *ſtruck*, may be as little as poſſible *ſhocked* with what is wonder-ful ! and without totally ſuppreſſing the deſcriptive circumſtances of the ſeveral *amours*, he ſo far has taken liberty with the original, as to purge them of a num-ber of indelicacies ; if notwithſtanding of which, ſome paſſages may ſtill be objected to, as rather luxuriant, the reader will at the ſame time perceive, that every irregular promptitude is al-ways cenſured by ſome moral reflection.

A KEY

A
KEY

TO THE

LIFE and CHARACTER

OF

MACBETH.

IN the profecution of this plan, as I fhall
confider it unneceffary to tire the reader
with tedious genealogical deductions, which
he may meet with in every general hiftory,
and which would render this work too vo-
luminous to anfwer the purpofe for which
it is intended; I will leave, therefore, all
the ordinary hiftorical occurrences to be
found in their proper places, and purfue
my defign, by entering immediately into
thofe particulars of each character which
are the moft entertaining, which may beft
exhibit the geniufes of my objects, and
fhew the connections and difpofitions which
induced poets to call them forth, as the moft
eligible fubjects for Theatrical Reprefenta-
-tions.   B   I,

It was in the 11th century, about the time of the expulsion of the *Danes*, and while *Edward* the Confessor reigned in *England*, that *Duncan* VII. reigned in *Scotland*.

Duncan was of too soft and easy a disposition to be at the head of a government divided into a diversity of factions, every one of which making advantage of their monarch's inactivity, laboured to aggrandize their several families, without any sort of regard to the public-weal. *Macbeth*, who was himself of the blood royal, who had more penetration, a quicker understanding, and a genius better suited for enterprizing, than any of his cotemporaries, became soon very conspicuous in this reign. His person was tall, but exactly proportioned ; he had a manly countenance, and from his eyes he darted so much of the awful and commanding spirit, as amongst all the other courtiers, seemed to indicate him the fittest for sway. To that manly deportment, which so distinguishingly secured him the respect of men, he could at pleasure accompany it with such a graceful and engaging address towards the ladies, as no less effectually recommended him to them : and as the gentler passions held, at the same time, a large place in his constitution, with those of a more ambitious and daring nature, whilst he commanded the

.vene-

veneration of the one sex, he rarely failed of insinuating himself into the approbation of the other. · So that, had the natural endowments of his mind and person been somewhat better tempered with the virtues of moderation and justice, and had he reached at the sceptre by no unfair means, as he was perfectly qualified to govern, and possessed every requisite talent to subdue the contentions which, in that reign of indolence, had distracted the people of his country, his name might have been transmitted to posterity with more of the Hero than the Tyrant.

In the same century, and before the reformations which were accomplished by the good king *Edward, England* had in like manner suffered by intestine divisions : and it being from some private memoirs of a noble family of this kingdom (*a*) that I have gathered many of the more genuine and interesting circumstances concerning the transactions, both in *England* and *Scotland,* for that æra, than I have found any where else ; so far as these relations shall appear to me to be more beautiful and natural than the accounts of other writers, I will stick pretty closely to them, and, regardless of what critics may say, I shall not blush, when I borrow materials as often as

---

(*a*) The noble family of **Howard.**

I can

I can see that my defign will thereby be improved.

Befides the memoirs already mentioned, accident flung into my hands the remains of fome old manufcripts found amongft charters and original papers, in the pof-feffion of one of the moft ancient families in *North Britain*, the old family of *Cummin*, now *Cumming* of *Altyre*. The authen-ticity of the manufcripts I do not take up-on me to eftablifh, any farther than from the probability which runs naturally through them, and that they reprefent a more in-terefting, as well as a much more enter-taining review of thefe times, than is to be collected from the many contradictory opi-nions of various authors who have hitherto treated of them.

It was in this reign, that *Edmund*, the reprefentative of one of the nobleft families in *England*, from the refentment of in-juftice which he conceived to have been done to himfelf and family, had abandoned the capital, and betaken himfelf, with his beloved fpoufe *Bertha*, to a retirement up-on the river *Ribble*, in *Lancafbire*, there to enjoy a more folid happinefs than he imagined could be found within the more fplendid circle of a court. It was in this peaceable retirement, that an accident in-tervened, which furnifhes a moft affecting, amufing,

amufing, and diftinct account of the intrigues of thefe days in the palaces of *Scotland*; and it is from that, compared with the manufcripts and other memoirs, that I propofe to prefent the reader with a relation of fuch circumftances as appear to be confiftent, in order to complete the illuftration of *Macbeth*'s enterprizes, character and reign.

One agreeable morning in the month of *May*, the fplendour of the rifing fun, fhooting forth his beams through the cleareft æther that poetic fancy can imagine, inviting the more temperate and fufficiently repofed of the human race, firft to glorify the Creator for their prefervation, and for the fecure enjoyment of that fweet repofe they have revived from; and next, to contemplate the various bounties of nature, juft frefhened by the vegetating moifture of night, now beginning, with opening foliage, to exult beneath the powerful rays of *Phœbus*: *Edmund*, with his amiable companion, had left their rural habitation, and by reciprocal meditations, felicitated each other, according to their daily cuftom, upon their undifturbed fituation; and to confirm a healthfulnefs, known only to innocence and fweet retirement, they now ftept forth to breathe the fragrance of the morning air. They purfued an agreeable

walk

walk towards the beach on the sea-side, which being here and there overhung by the natural ruins of some shaggy rocks, at the same time diversified and beautified the rural landskip of their delightful abode. The sea was then in a profound calm, and but by a superior clearnefs and extenſion, ſcarcely diſtinguiſhed itself from the ſtilleſt lake. By the now ſo tranquil borders of that ſometimes ſo noiſy and bluſtering element, this happy pair courted the refreſhing breezes, which then ſkimmed to them from alongſt its ſurface; until the advancing ſun, having gathered yet increaſing ſtrength, began to convince them of the inſtability of every human enjoyment, by incommoding them with the warmth of thoſe very beams which had, a very little while ago, been their pleaſure and admiration! They therefore looked about them for a ſheltering retreat, and were quickly invited to one, under the cover of a ſhading rock, which was alternately paved with ſoft moſs, adorned with wild and wandering flowers, odoriferous herbs, and variegated ſhrubs, irregularly nodding over its impending parts. In this ſhade, invited to ſympathetic colloquy,— ‘ O my dear *Edmund*, (began *Bertha*) how much happier are we in this virtuous retirement, than in all the falſe ſplendour of a court,

‘ where

' where ambition, envy, malice and felf-
' intereft, formed into bafe plots, never
' fuffer true pleafure to tranquilize thofe
' deluded fools, who there court their own
' undoing ?"——— ' The purfuit of man-
' kind, my beloved *Bertha*, (replied the
' grave *Edmund*) is as contradictory and
' abfurd, as were the debates of the old
' philofophers about their fupreme good !
' One places it in pleafure, another in
' health, a third in dignities, and a fourth
' in power ! Thus every one gives it chace
' by different, yet by devious ways, while
' none come in with the quarry, all having
' miftaken the fcent ; confulting more their
' paffions than their reafon, they always
' magnify the idea, and fo greatly heighten
' the defire, that difappointment attends
' even the fuccefs of their wifhes !——But
' we having conquered thofe wandering
' and uncertain hopes, which depend on
' things without us, confine our happinefs
' to our prefent poffeffions, to thofe virtues
' which we cherifh in our own breafts, and
' which, under the benign influence of an
' approving Deity, ripens into thofe real
' pleafures, which, without the vitiated
' palate of ambition, we now begin to
' tafte of ; wifely proving to ourfelves this
' religious truth, that even oppreffion,
' affliction and difappointment, may lead
' into

' into the road of happinefs.'———In this fenfible and confoling manner, were this amiable and contented couple congratulating each other on their prefent enjoyments, and fo entirely intent on the fubject of their felicity, that while they yet difcourfed, they were inattentive to a fudden change which had now ftolen upon the face of nature, as if it had been exprefs, to furnifh them with another recent proof of that ficklenefs and uncertainty which wait upon all earthly ferenity. A chilnefs, which had crept gradually, and almoft infenfibly, upon them, ftopt the courfe of converfation, and they were now about removing from the rocky fhelter, when they perceived, that the late fo placid countenances of both fea and air looked more denfe and gloomy; the fwelling furges began, in murmurs, to quicken their advances to the beach, affumed the form of waves, and foon, with hoarfer grumblings, dafhed with vain fury, fucceffively, againft the founding fhore !—— The fky loft, almoft imperceptibly, its native azure, and was forming into more angry looking clouds, which rifing progreffively from the limited horizon, now fpread with obfcurity the whole expanfe ! an unformed rain, fputter'd, as if it were in combat with the winds, which, from uncouth whiftling, fwelled to frightful bluftering.

ing, and at length seemed to hurry balls of fire and fury throughout the convulsed atmosphere! contending, seemingly, with the roused, rolling, roaring element below, which should strike with mightiest horrors the astonished mortals!

Edmund and *Bertha* now bethought themselves how they might best escape the effects of such an awful storm: they had sauntered too far from their house, and were fain to regain their covert in the rock, into which, penetrating a little farther, they found a safe protection from the inclemency of the tempest, and had still an opportunity of viewing its terrors in perspective.

After having been cooped up in this cave for more than an hour, they imagined they spied at a distance the appearance of a vessel struggling with the jarring billows; but as this figure was as often buried in the voids, formed between the high-swelled waves, as it could be sometimes discerned on the surface, their notions about it were yet only conjectural; but as the wind blew from the sea, and the half-wreck'd vessel disdaining the power of navigation, they could perceive that every violent gust forced the object nearer and nearer to their eye, until at length they could plainly discover her to be a galley, in every agony of distress;

diſtreſs; and ſoon the lamentable ſkrieks of perſishing mortals affectingly aſſailed their pitying ears, when, more earneſt for the preſervation of their fellow creatures, than anxious about their own ſafety, they abandoned their covert, and fighting through the ſtorm, haſtened to the ſea-ſide, which they had hardly gained, when, dreadful to relate! the bottom, which until then had baffled the force of concuſſive billows, yielded to the quicker ſhock of a hidden bank, and ſoon was ſcattered in divided pieces! The pitying ſpectators, filled with every compaſſionate emotion, vainly riſked their own ſafety, by ſometimes mingling with the ſpent fury of the waves, the ſooner to ſtretch forth their willing arms for the relief of ſome ſuffering mortals, whom they could now diſtinguiſh had clung themſelves to different pieces of the ſeparated wreck; when looking round them, and the obſcurity of the ſky now giving place again to a more reviving light, they obſerved, not far from them, too venerable forms, like hermits, who ſeemed to have come down to the beach, and to be waiting, with the ſame heavenly intention to adminiſter, if poſſible, medicine to the diſtreſſed. Some mariners who by ſtrength and habit were abler to labour againſt the waves, firſt found their ſafety on the welcome ſhore, and

and were comforted by the united endeavours of those who hospitably waited
for the occasion. But now the eyes of the
pitying *Edmund* and his consort were fixed
upon a plank, which they had discovered
to be still labouring with the storm, and
yet in a situation almost hopeless, and upon
which they imagined they also saw some
human figures. The manly *Edmund* could
not long be the beholder only of such imminent hazard, but in he plunges among
the waves, leaving the trembling *Bertha*'s
soul divided between blame on the rashness
of her love, and the hopes of seeing him
accomplish what he so generously dared;
whilst he, having exerted the power of
every nerve, approached the unwieldy
plank, gained the farthest side of it, and
dextrously pushed it to the beach before
him. What words can paint the lively joy
which soon dispelled the palid fears which
had so expressively distinguished themselves
o'er every feature of the lovely *Bertha*, now
not only blessed in the safe return of her
dearest *Edmund*; but having seen him, by
an uncommon exertion of a native resolution, be the happy preserver of a wreck,
richly freighted with a venerable looking
old gentleman, (*a*) one younger, (*b*) and

(*a*) Thane of Angus. (*b*) Lorn, son to the thane
of Argyle.

a beautiful young lady, (*a*) whofe appear-
ances, under all their diftrefs, indicated
every one of them to be noble.

The good Hermits, not altogether ftrangers to the like woeful cataftrophies, were
provided with cordials, well calculated for
fuch affecting occafions, by the virtues of
which, and the returning influence of the
fun, which had at length triumphed over
the fudden and violent invafions of the
tempeft, the youngeft gentleman began to
fhew figns of unextinguifhed life : opening
his eyes, and awakening as it were from
the flumber of death, he fighed out, O!
my *Eugenia!*—my *Eugenia!* have I loft
thee, and do I live?——*Eugenia*, who had
been no lefs the care of *Bertha*, and one of
the Hermits, began alfo to move with the
reviving pulfations of life, and uttered
faintly, in faultering accents,—O! my foul!
my love! my *Lorn!* where art thou? Far
thou can'ft not be! We were too clofely
linked together for fate to part us!——The
found, indiftinct as it was, catched the
ready ears of *Lorn*, and his eyes foon turned
to whence it came. The unfolding lids of
Eugenia's, made her's now meet the opened
eyes of *Lorn!* They looked, fouls full of

(*a*) Angus's daughter.

thank-

thankfulnefs towards their deliverers; and
had once more well nigh loft their fight,
by the overflowings of love, in gazing
wonder, inexpreffible! at one another!——
But haftening too faft to banifh every doubt
of their yet fearcely credited exiftence,
they hurried to embrace, and funk into one
another's arms with fuch extreme emotion,
that reftoring cordials were again as neceffary as before. Again adminiftered! again
revived! Say, how emphatically the horrors of the paft tempeft were now contrafted
by the delicatenefs of all that's tender?

Eugenia's returning fenfes had but juft
affured her of her own, and of her beloved's
fafety, when, with ftill the look of uncompleted life, fhe tenderly enquired, if any
thing had been feen of a reverend old gentleman, who had been a companion in their
fate? for alas! added fhe, how greatly
damped fhall be the prefent hour of joy, if
it is to be lowered with the lofs of a father?
Age, not fo well able to ftruggle with fa-
tigues as youth, had rendered the recovery
of the old gentleman more difficult than
that of either *Lorp* or *Eugenia*; but the
other Hermit, who had adminiftered every
poffible application to him, finding his revival yet precarious, was now befeeching
more affiftance, and every one more eager
than another, haftened with help, till at
C length,

length, by chafing his temples, and forcing restoratives down his throat, he began also to shew marks of returning life ; to sustain which, however, it was plain, that some place more comfortable than the open beach was immediately necessary. The house of *Edmund* was too far off, and no convenient place so near as the cottage of the Hermits, where, although there were no extraordinary accommodations to be had, yet there were sufficient to procure for him some immediate repose, and such refreshment as might sooner enable him to proceed a little farther into the country.

The men all joined in helping the old gentleman up the cliffs, and to support him, until they arrived at a neat hut, the cleanly dwelling of our supposed Anchorites. *Eugenia* followed, accompanied by the hospitable *Bertha*. And now our whole company having entered the hermitage, a fire is quickly lighted up, the old gentleman placed near it, his wet garments removed, and supplied with such other apparel as the cottage could afford ; whilst the considerate *Edmund* posted home to his house, and was not tardy in returning with dry cloathing also for the fair *Eugenia*, and her *Lorn*, neither of whom could be prevailed with to leave the hermitage, until they could see the old gentleman in so promising

ising

mifing a way, as to be accounted out of
danger. Pain, and the extremity to which
he had been reduced, had rendered him fo
pale, and had fo much altered his look,
that a moft intimate acquaintance could
with difficulty have known him ; yet *Edmund* and *Bertha*, as he began to recover
could not avoid obferving, that one of the
Hermits had eyed him with uncommon
eagernefs, and that whilft he gazed at him,
fymptoms of ftifled anger, indignation,
hatred and revenge, were to be read in his
difordered countenance ! But how foon, by
the heat of the fire, dry covering, by
repeated cordials, and other refrefhing reftoratives, he began to re-affume his natural graceful appearance, the hitherto fmothered refentment of the Anchorite boiled
up into the moft violent rage ; and juft as
the half-recovered old man was collecting
the faculties of fpeech, and had begun to
exprefs his gratitude to Heaven, and to his
prefervers, the incenfed Hermit indignantly
interrupted him ;— ' By Heaven, (fays he)
' it is he ! it is that very villain ! that devil
' incarnate ! that accurfed minifter and ad-
' vifer to the vileft of all tyrants, *Macbeth !*
' How juft, oh! ye heavenly powers, do
' ye prove yourfelves in all your works !
' and in none of them more than this !—
' By

' By sending this monster to suffer that pu-
' nishment, by my hands, which he owes
' to myself, to my family, and to ten thou-
' sand more!——Look on me, *Angus!* and
' to thy confusion! recollect, under this
' disguise, the so much injured *Glamis!*
' that same *Glamis*, who has been affronted,
' ruined, and, to save that life so anxiously
' persued, now driven from my native
' country, to waste out the miserable re-
' mains of it in hated exile, and all by thy
' damnable counsel to the most profligate
' of all tyrants! Behold in that wretch,
' ye generous *English!* the most wicked,
' the most abandoned of the human race!
' the bane and destruction of his conntry!
' the ruin of her ancient nobles! the op-
' pressor of her people! and the instru-
' ment, in the impious hands of *Macbeth,*
' of butchering the laws and liberties of
' *Scotland!*' With these last words he un-
sheathed a dagger, and, but for the timely
interposition of the amazed company, he
had instantly plunged it in the heart of
Angus. Fear and filial piety threw the beautiful *Eugenia* between her father and the
intended blow; and love soon shot the
stunned *Lorn* between the Thane and his
beloved; and directing his more nervous
arm to the hand of the furious *Glamis*, he
thence, with difficulty, wrested the threaten-
ing

ing dagger ; and now recognizing *Glamis*, whom he did not fooner know,—— ' Hold
' noble Thane! (faid the agitated youth)
' Great as thy injuries have been, let not
' the remembrance of them make thee fall
' below thyfelf, below the reputation of
' thy arms, of thy honour and virtue ; by
' hurrying out of life an old, weak, and
' already half dead gentleman ; who, if he
' has been guilty of the crime imputed to
' him, has, by a variety of fufferings, in
' fome degree attoned for them. Far from
' now approving of the arbitrary and cruel
' meafures exercifed by *Macbeth*, or jufti-
' fying the feeming participation that his
' fituation expofed him to in thefe tranfac-
' tions, he reflects upon them with fincere
' contrition : and fuppofing him to be as
' criminal as you imagine him, and totally
' in your power, yet furely it would be
' more in character for the noble *Glamis* to
' confent that he live to wafh off that guilt
' with his tears, which you would rafhly
' punifh with his blood. Know, *Glamis*,
' (added he) that although I am not un-
' acquainted with the dreadful accufations
' with which his country have blamed him,
' yet at the fame time I know that his foul
' is poffeffed of virtues, which the times
' and the jealoufy of the tyrant did not per-
' mit him to enforce. Be therefore, thou

generous,

generous, injured Thane! perfuaded to
command thy awakened vengeance, nor
put me to the reluctant neceffity of oppofing where I have fo much refpect;
for affure thyfelf, that while *Lorn* has
any blood in his veins, none fhall now
come at the life of *Angus*, but through
the heart of *Lorn!*' ' Prodigious! (replied the ftill enraged *Glamis*) what
ftrange degeneracy? What unparallelled
bafenefs? The young *Lorn* to protect
that guilty head, by whofe advice his
own father was treacheroufly murdered!
by whom his relations are robbed of their
eftates! and thofe who could efcape the
dagger or the poifon, forced, like me, to
wander into foreign lands, and to fubfift
on the pitying charity of ftrangers! Is
it poffible, that any of the generous blood
of the great houfe of *Argyle* remains to
circulate in thy veins, and thou declare
thyfelf the protector of the bafe inftrument by which thy family has been fo
exceedingly oppreffed! Say, was not
Angus the very active foul of *Macbeth*?
Did that infernal ufurper perpetrate any
mifchief, or did he contrive the ruin of
any noble patriot, without firft confulting his concurring oracle, the bafe *Angus?*
Oh! *Lorn!* thou beareft the image of thy
dear murdered father in thy face! ba-
' ftardize

' ftardize not thyfelf, nor degenerate from
' that noble line and principle, which have
' been fo long illuftrious for virtue and for
' honour !'

Embarraffed as the much affected *Lorn*
now ftood before the wondering *Edmund*,
Bertha, the other attentive Hermit, and
the indignant trembling *Eugenia*; recol-
lecting himfelf, with an equal mixture of
modefty and grandeur, he thus anfwered
to the ftinging reproaches of the venerable
Glamis: ' If I fhould not be able to juftify
' my honour, and yet defend the life of
' the father of my dear *Eugenia*, I will fa-
' crifice both to the feverity of your juftice.
' But be firft a juft judge, lay afide paffion,
' which never attends the ear of equity ;
' and with cool impartiality hear me plead
' the caufe I am efpoufing.'

The compaffionating hearts of *Edmund*
and the real Hermit were greatly moved
with the expreffivenefs which appeared on
both fides of this affecting fcene ; whilft
Bertha's feelings for the labouring diftreffes
of the fair *Eugenia*, reprefented her as fo
much a fharer in her anxiety, that the
noble *Edmund*, willing to put an end to
fuch a melancholy altercation, now interpofed ; and addreffing himfelf to the exafperated *Glamis*, delivered himfelf to this
effect: That it was not now the time to

difcufs the intricacies of a queftion, which appeared to be fo important to the interefts of both the parties; that to complete a perfect recovery from thofe unfpeakable dangers from which thofe of one fide had been fo lately and fo providentially relieved, it was yet neceffary that they fhould be accommodated with many other reftoratives; and that for his part, he fhould not admit, that the rules of hofpitality, which now lay at his door to give proofs of, fhould be fo unreafonably tranfgreffed upon, as to be fo immediately interrupted with family contentions; and he hoped that the worthy *Glamis* would, for the prefent at leaft, fubdue the rifings of private revenge, as not confiftent with his own good underftanding, nor juftifiable by the laws of the land they had come to feek protection in. Thefe remonftrances, which were gravely feconded by the real Hermit, who reafoned alfo from motives of Chriftianity, which difcountenance revenge of any fort, as totally repugnant to the precepts of that pure religion which ought to be the guide and conductor of all our actions. By the joint arguments of thefe worthy perfons, the lately aroufed anger of the vindictive *Glamis* began to be appeafed; and the fenfible heart of the abafhed and yet weakly *Angus* was full with what it had in vain laboured to difcharge,

difcharge, and which the confiderate *Edmund*, for this time, put a ftop to; and having provided proper carriages for the purpofe, they were all feverally conducted to the hofpitable poffeffions of their generous protector.

The falutary and kind entertainment which the ftrangers found in the affectionate applications of *Edmund* and *Bertha*, procured a repofe fo reftorative to them, that the next day they were furprifingly recovered ; and even the old Thane of *Angus* was fo much revived, that he was in a condition to receive the congratulations of every one who condefcended to vifit him ; but of all the reft, he being the moft anxious to fee the Thane of *Glamis*, he firft expreffed his defire to be tranfported to the Hermits cave ; but every body, from regard for him, oppofing that attempt, as yet hazardous ; *Edmund*, with the brother Hermit, walked out, and fo fuccefsfully expoftulated with *Glamis*, that he was at length prevailed on to accompany them in a vifit to *Angus*, who no fooner beheld him in his apartment, the frowns which he wore on his countenance the preceding day, being a good deal foftened, than with an air of noble complacency he thus accofted him :—— ' So generous a vifit to ' the man whom I confefs you have but
' too

'too much reason to hate, touches me
'much more sensibly than all those re-
'proaches with which you loaded me at
'our last meeting: I wish for nothing
'more than to convince you, that although
'every appearance, from a too blind obe-
'dience to a tyrannical master, is much
'against me; yet if you will condescend to
'hearken with patience to the secret history
'of these times, and will judge candidly of
'the motives which originally engaged me
'into that diabolical service, from which
'I never had it till now in my power to re-
'tire with safety, I flatter myself, that even
'the just and rigid *Glamis*, if he cannot
'approve, will at least excuse in me the
'involuntary administration of many enor-
'mities, which were repugnant to my na-
'ture, but to which I was obliged to lend
'my name, or, by my own untimely death,
'make place for some wickeder minister,
'who might not study so much as I did to
'season cruelty with moderation.' The
offended *Glamis*, who could not yet conquer entirely his indignation, was, however,
extremely disposed to hear an account of
the strange transactions which had passed
in his native country, to which, since his
unhappy banishment, he had been so totally
a stranger; and well knowing that no other
person was capable to give so exact a history
of

of them, he in the mean time difguifed his refentment; and fignifying to *Angus*, that he would liften with great attention to his relation, *Angus* was happy in the condefcenfion; but as the day was rather too far fpent, and he yet too weak to undertake fo interefting a tafk, he propofed, that all the gentlemen fhould next morning meet in his apartment, and that then he would gratify them with the knowledge of fuch tranfactions as would amaze them to hear, and fadly affect him to relate; but fuggefting that, as for the fake of truth, he fhould be obliged to difplay many intrigues, plots and cabals, rather improper for gentle ears, he defired that the ladies, efpecially his daughter *Eugenia*, as too much perfonally concerned in fome of them, might contrive for themfelves fome other amufement.

Every member of this little company was more impatient than another, until the hour fhould arrive that was to bring them together the next morning. The Thane of *Angus* was prepared for the meeting, and how foon they were convened, and the common falutations of the day performed, he proceeded with great precifion and fenfibility through the following affecting and interefting circumftances.

'I being five years older than *Macbeth*, my appearance in the court of King *Duncan*

was

was very nigh by fo much earlier than his;
and as I myfelf had met with no unfavourable reception, but was rather regarded as
one of the foremoft in the courtly circle, I
had a fhare in *Macbeth*'s introduction, while
he was yet but one and twenty years of age.
His noble and fprightly deportment gained
a prejudice in his favour with both fexes;
and I cannot help acknowledging, that he
foon made very ftrong impreffions upon
me. At that æara there feemed to be a
fimilarity in our difpofitions, which in a
manner pre-occupied one another's approbation. We were both tinctured with ambition, but as that had not then rifen to
fuch a pitch of predominance, as to fubdue
fofter paffions, we had at the fame time no
fmall propenfity to the amorous. It was
therefore, that in the commencement of our
acquaintance, the greateft fhare of our in-
duftry was devoted to love; and intriguing
with the ladies, employed, in thefe days,
more of our time than the intrigues of the
ftate.

' Amongft all the fair who adorned this
court, none fhone with fo much influence
as the two lately married daughters of the
Thane of *Broad-Albain*, *Jaquenetta* and *Anabella*. The firft was wife to the Thane of
Gaurey, and the other to the Thane of *Kyle*,
who were both men of power in the court;
but

Gaurey, and the other to the Thane of *Kyle*, who were both men of power at court; but being much more advanced in years than their ladies, and not supposed equal to those fires, which the addresses of the gay and gallant, with youth, were likely to inspire in the breasts of young persons of their beauty and quality; these amiable creatures were greatly exposed to the artillery of sweet hearts, better suited to their years. *Jaquenetta* had, I blush to confess it, kindled a flame in my heart, which I had not virtue enough to subdue; and *Anabella* it seemed had made no less impression in the breast of *Macbeth*.—It would be to give my relation, too much the air of romance, to be particular in the various stratagems we employed to seduce them, and of the success which both of us at length had our applications crowned with; let it suffice to inform you, that our assiduity met with no unfavourable reception, that in a short time we were happy to our wish; and that it was perhaps owing to the connections in these amours, and to some circumstances attending them, that first created a confidence, and at last insensibly, formed such a league, between *Macbeth* and me, as it was hardly possible to dissolve."

D

It

" It would be, continued the Thane, as unfuitable at my time of life, as it is inconfiftent with my prefent way of thinking, to entertain you my friends, with tales of love, and yet as they are in fome refpect neceffary to elucidate the contradictions of which fo fingular a character was compofed; here you will find the account of *Macbeth's* intrigue with Lady *Kyle*, as taken from his own diction, for in thefe days we were fo entirely impregnated with a mutual approbation, that we began this ftrong inftance of it, I by recording the relation he gave of his affair with *Anabella*, and he of mine with her fifter, and it will probably aftonifh you to obferve, that a man fo fufceptible of the finer touches of amour, could be poffeffed of a foul fo capable of rapacity and tyranny. It is true, thefe amours were founded in guilt, and it is with remorfe I now own it, that even the fofteft paffion when infpired by criminality can only find room in fuch breafts as are open to other vices; the influence they had in fubfequent tranfactions makes it neceffary to mention them, and your reading them over will be a remiffion to me from the fatigue of the narration." *Edmund* took the paper and from thence continued the detail as if there had been no interruption.

Macbeth

" *Macbeth* one night, having an affignation
with *Anabella*, to which for the fake of both
her's, and his own reputation no mortal was
privy, he went alone to the rendezvous:
he was waiting for the agreed fignal, by
the fide of a garden wall, when his liften-
ing ears catched the alarm of fome perfons,
as if advancing from another quarter ; he
fought in a void by the garden door to
conceal himfelf, in hopes thofe whom
he judged to be approaching, might in the
dark pafs by, without difcovering him ;
but contrary to his expectation, they took
poft juft by him; and then he heard one
of the company, thus, accoft the reft——
" Watch this poft with all care, it cannot
be long 'ere he come ; my intelligence is
certain ; and how foon he appears, be it
your care to prevent his efcaping, and
thereby to have in his power the difcovery
of our enterprize.——Befides the reward I
have promifed, you will have the fatisfaction of punifhing a man, who has injured yourfelves, by having obtained thofe
places once enjoyed by you, for fome of
his own creatures ; when he is difpatched,
thefe places, will be in my father's power,
you know my influence with him, and you
may rely upon my ufing it for men, who
by the deftruction, of my preferred rival,
fhall open for me a lefs interrupted paffage

 to

to the dear object of my paffion."—*Macbeth* immediately diftinguifhed by the voice, that this cowardly harrangue was uttered, by no other than *Thurfo*, fon to the old Thane of *Caithnefs*, whom he knew to be not only his rival in the love of *Anabella*, but one who had fruitlefly difputed the King's favour, with him; but how it was poffible for him, to preferve both reputation and perfon, in fuch a terrible dilemma, where his fingle arm muft be oppofed, to thofe of three or four; he knew not.—— *Thurfo* who had no mind to be known in this dirty matter himfelf, having employed three of the moft worthlefs of his clan, who had for different malverfations been difmiffed from offices they enjoyed under the crown, and for which deprivation he had influenced them to blame *Macbeth*, he, I fay, withdrew after the delivery of his charge to them; and they in looking about for the moft retired corner to conceal themfelves in, were entering the very porch, where *Macbeth* was hid, when inftantly unfheathing his fword, he fuddenly leaped through them, and gained a more open fituation; the affaffins purfued, and at once he had all the three fwords pointed againft him; to fuch a fuperiority, he muft no doubt have foon fubmitted with his life, had it not happened to be my good, or rather ill, fortune,
having

having that very moment, left lefs interrupted joys in the arms of *Jaquenetta*, who
lived in a houfe almoft adjoining to her
fifter's ; had it not happened, I fay to be my
fortune to arrive in the inftant.——I did not
immediately know *Macbeth*, nor had then
any remarkable intimacies paffed between
us ; but the inequality of the engagement,
and the apparent barbarity of the affault,
foon determined me, on which fide to join
my endeavours : I drew my fword, and
placing myfelf clofe by *Macbeth*, bid him
fear nothing from fuch aggreffors, for the
bafe hearts, that had been capable of at-
tacking a fingle gentleman, would certainly
be forced to fubmit to the more generous,
and united ftrength of two honeft men!——
I had fcarcely faid fo much, when, as if
my words and prefence had infpir'd him
with frefh vigour, he made a furious pafs,
and laid one of the three ruffians dead at
our feet : the other two, having now neither
the advantage of numbers, nor of a good
caufe, began to fave themfelves by flight ;
but *Thurfo* who waited the event, at no
great diftance ; and whofe refentment againft
Macbeth, was, by the defeat of his bravadoes rather aggravated than abated, interrupted their efcape, and upbraiding their
daftardlinefs, had the impudence, with
fword in hand, to lead them back himfelf

D 3

to the base affaffination : *Macbeth* ftood upon his defence, and by an artful addrefs to
the ruffians, and intreating me not to difhonour any more my fword, in combating
with affaffins, he perfwaded them to defift,
and to let the young *Caithnefs* prove himfelf worthy or not, of the prize he courted,
by contending it with him fingly : it was
impoffible, in fuch a fituation, for *Thurfo*
to fhun the challenge, and therefore, now
fummoning all the falfe courage he was
mafter of, in aid of his revenge, he affaulted
the more dextrous *Macbeth* with every mark
of fury; but he was quickly convinced of
his antagonift's fuperiority, by receiving
from his fword fuch a defperate wound, as
in an inftant, made him tumble at his feet :
and could now only gratify his difappointed
wrath, in growling imprecations upon the
head of his conqueror; and againft the too
lovely, but partial *Anabella !—Macbeth*
threatened by another ftab, to punifh his
bafenefs, and to put it out of his power, to
give any account of the caufe of his fall,
fo as to injure the peace and reputation
of *Anabella*; but upon my remonftrating,
that to repeat the wounds he had fo fairly
given, while the other was in a ftate of defence, would now that he lay defencelefs on
the ground, be deemed unworthy of him, and
give rife to calumny; he was eafily prevailed

vailed with ; and thus *Thurfo* was left to
the care of his two ruffians, who we imagined were not far off, although fear had
removed them from our view.—I offered to
attend *Macbeth* to his apartments, which he
willingly accepted of, for although till now
he had not been fenfible of them, yet in
the fury of *Thurfo*'s firft onfet, he had
given him two flight wounds, one of which
bleeding pretty plentifully, had rendered
him fomewhat faintifh ; I fupported him
home, fent immediately for a furgeon, and
amidft a thoufand expreffions of the warmeft
gratitude, I waited till his wounds were
dreffed, and as there was no fort of danger
in them, I left him to his repofe.—I went
next morning to enquire how he did, he received me with numberlefs careffes, faid I
was his preferver, and affured me that while
he lived, he would ftudy to convince me of
the deep fenfe he had of the fervice I had done
him : in fine, there appeared to be fo much
fincerity, and cordiality in the fentiments of
gratitude, with which he then courted my
friendfhip, that I fhall confefs he excited in
me a prejudice in his favour, which exceeded any thing, I had ever to that hour
felt for mankind ; fuch a mutual approbation of one another, could not fail to grow
up to fuch a confidence, as produced that
fingular union and amity, which bound me
in

in connections with him, so much longer than his actions, with remorse I acknowledge it, deserved the countenance of the patriot or honest man.———Having upon this occasion however, reciprocally exchanged engagements of the most inviolable friendship ; I will not delay, my dear preserver, said he, to give you the strongest testimony, that one man is capable of giving to another, of that confidence, which I think you only deserve, by communicating to you a secret which no person on earth knows, or should ever know from me but yourself ; although from what happened last night, I am afraid the charming *Anabella* through some fatal necessity, must have trusted it with some confidante of hers. It is, my dear friend, on account of a preference which that matchless creature has bless'd me with ; that the ambitious, tho' cowardly, son of *Caithness* has been provoked to enterprize the scene of baseness which you found him employed in ; and by what I heard him say, as he charged his meaner souled instruments, with the execution of his unmanly purpose, I dread, I say, that *Anabella* must have been betrayed by some one, who for our conveniency, she may have trusted with the important secret.——This darling *Anabella*, the beautiful wife of the old Thane of *Kyle*, cannot have escap'd the eyes of a nobleman of *Angus*'s

Angus's penetration : and although it be true, that fhe has birth, merit, and above all, beauty, which better entitle her to the arms of the greateft monarch on earth, than to the feeble embraces of an old Thane, or to be miftrefs to the moft accomplifhed of the human race ; yet, my worthy friend, fo amazingly fortunate have I been, as to have rendered myfelf agreeable to that charmer ; and with her, when occafion can be found, to revel in fuch tranfports, as fhe alone can beftow.—Yet thefe delights, of which *Anabella* herfelf would now be no churl, are, like every thing elfe that's rare, not to be purchafed without difficulties : The hufband, rather uxorious, than otherwife, has few avocations abroad, and thofe he has, are fo uncertain, that fometimes interruption itfelf, and fometimes the fear of it, have hitherto prevented my being regaled with a belly-full of Love.——Permit me, continued *Macbeth*, to divert you for a moment, with fome comical enough circumftances which attended our immediately preceding difappointment : *Anabella* had kindly fent me notice that her Thane was juft preparing to go upon a vifit, at fuch a diftance from home, as fhe imagined would detain him till the next day, and that in any event, fhe thought we might, with fafety, pafs fome moments together, that afternoon : You will not, my dear friend, believe

believe that I flighted fo defirable an invitation; I waited, or more properly lingered, with the utmoft impatience, until the appointed minute arrived, and then with all the ardour of enthufiaftic love: I haftened me to the field of beauty! And there!—'tis yet a heaven to relate it! I found, the charmer of my foul, in a negligent, but bewitching undrefs; through the flim elegance of which, the perfect proportion of every part, fwelling upon the imagination, commanded by irrefiftible attraction, an admiration not to be awakened by all the pomp, which drefs can borrow from embroidery or jewels!—It muft be the moft luxuriant fancy, and not words, that can defcribe to you, the thrilling emotions which now circulated thro' every Member of the enchanted *Macbeth!* to be fhort, after fully feafting my ravifhed eyes, and gratifying every amorous touch; I had juft plunged into fruition! when O! more than cruel intervention! the voice of the old Thane ftartled us from a neighbouring chamber!—and forced me, reluctant, to retire, and raging, leave the uncompleted banquet!—Danger inevitable now confounded both!—hardly one moment for confideration! fo that I thought of no other refource than, by my fword, to gain our immediate deliverance.—But happily for the Thane, and

no.

no lefs fortunate for us, the lucky accident of fearching for what he had forgotten detained him fome minutes in the antichamber; this gave the half diftracted *Anabella* time to recover her fcattered fenfes, the confequence of which was, that fhe directed me, to creep immediately under the bed as the only hiding place our fituation afforded; I however without either thought or hefitation inftantly complied; and had juft fquatted in my irkfome retreat, and fhe but half adjufted, when in entered the unfufpecting Thane : *Anabella* had placed herfelf on the couch, the better to conceal any impreffions, which might have been vifible there : he appeared at firft furprized; and afked her, Why in that undrefs ?——She anfwered with amazing readinefs; that the day had been intolerably hot; and that as he had gone from home, fhe was determined to fee no company; fhe intended therefore to dream away the fultry hours, in refrefhing flumbers. and had unrob'd herfelf, for her more eafy repofe.——The inviting difhabile, and engaging attitude, he found her in, even began to quicken unufual emotions in the grave Thane; he feated himfelf by her, and became a recent proof, that fuch exquifite charms as the tempting *Anabella* poffeffed, could invigorate the half chilled faculties of age itfelf:

in

In fine, profiting of the privileges of a husband, he proceeded to amuse himself with liberties which she would fain have dispensed with, and which were to me as shocking, as a view of the happiness of the first human pair, was to the sight of the envying devil. She used every means her art could suggest, to postpone at least, an enjoyment, which at that juncture must be the more disgustful to herself, as she knew it would be tormenting to me: she affected indisposition, assumed a countenance of ill humour ; she struggled ; she scolded ; but as every opposition serves rather to whetten than abate the amorous rage, so it was with old *Kyle*, whose eagerness increasing by resistance, at length matrimonially laboured, to perform the office of a lover ! Whilst the unwilling *Anabella*, submitting to the authority of a husband, in the same instant that she gave pleasure to one who was then very indifferent to her, was extended tortures to the man she loved!——Patience however, having endured the conjugal conflict, and the Thane's unfinished business still waiting for him at a distance, he was obliged to retire ; although he was on this occasion so remarkably enamoured of the degagée air he catched *Anabella* in, that he embraced her at parting with uncommon ardour, promised (what she could have excused him from).

from) not to fleep from home if poffible, and finally, curfed that bufinefs which fhould ever make it neceffary for him, to to be an hour abfent from fo delightful a companion."

' Loofely attired as fhe was, fhe attended him down ftairs, not fo much from regard or compliment, as to fee him remount his fteed, and be thereby affured that he was really gone. She quickly reafcended and having fecured all the doors, approached with moft compaffionating complacency to welcome my enlargement from that ungracious confinement, out of which I had juft emerged.—A concioufnefs of her having been the reluctant inftrument of fo much torment to a perfon beloved by her, overfpread her lovely countenance with the moft expreffive blufhes; O! do not hate me, my dear *Macbeth*, faid fhe, for what I could not help, confiftently with your fafety; for believe me, my Lord, my anxiety to fupprefs every appearance of fufpicion, and to fhorten the moments of your difmal confinement, had more prevalence over my involuntary mind, than all the arguments of conjugal authority. I haftily caught her in my arms, and interrupted her with glowing kiffes! To hate you, I anfwered, is impoffible! But O! how much more than ever do I hate your

E   detefted

deteſted huſband! O! may the more generous beaſt he rides revenge my quarrel, and by a well-timed toſs, ſo effectually diſable him, that he may never be again in a capacity to rifle thoſe ſweets, which were beſtowed for the bleſſings of youth, and not to be abuſed by the inſipid pawings of old age.——But no more of the baneful ſubject.——Let us now rekindle the more equal flames of love, and drown all thought of care in currents of ſubſtantial joy!——No! ſaid *Anabella*, I will not give pollution to the arms I love! I will follow the uſage of the ancients, and by ablution cleanſe me of the ſtains I've ſuffered!——So ſaying, ſhe diſengaged herſelf from the cloſe embrace, and hurrying through different apartments, at laſt unfolding a double door, ſhe threw aſide her looſe attire, and plunged into a well prepared bath. The floating beauties which now inflamed my agitated ſoul, enhanced, if poſſible, the extacy I had felt before!——All patience left me; I rather tore than pulled off my clothes, and ruſhed into this new, this liquid ſcene of love! If ever you have ſeen the genuine tranſports of the ſwelling necked ſwans, when prompted by genial inſtinct to frolick on the ſuſtaining ſurface of the ſtream, how they bill and twine, and twine and bill, and proudly expand the wings of gladneſs which

which they feel! So were the joyous embraces of my love and me! Like them too we might have sported longer, but the more delicate frame of the lovely *Anabella* being the firſt ſuſceptible of the too cooling element, began, by gentle ſhiverings, to intimate an inclination to change the ſcene. I ſupported her to the ſteps on the farther ſide, where towels, and other conveniencies for the occaſion, were to be found. We performed, with mutual tranſports, the offices of bathing waiters for each other, and I ſoon revived in my lovely *Naied* thoſe warm circulations, which had for a little time been chilled. She attired herſelf as before; and, taught by her example, I rather hung my veſtments over me than put them on. The nymph, reflective, viewed with approving bluſhes the unmeditated novelty of the ſcene, and every beauty of the lovely image was thereby amazingly improved; in this fulneſs of delight, I led her, unreluctant, through the different paſſages, and regained the apartment firſt deſigned for amorous ſport; and there, in extacies unutterable, we re-communicated reciprocal delights! —— Unwilling, yet, to caſt a thought on thoſe hours ſo pleaſantly ſpent in amorous dalliance, the evening's duſk, however, gave us warning, that mutual ſafety demanded we ſhould part: full

time

time it was, for I had not proceeded many
yards from the feat of all my joy, when I
could perceive the cheated Thane advancing to his houfe.——— A tedious week has
paffed fince that delightful day ; and until
yefterday, it had not been in *Anabella's*
power to blefs me with another opportunity : it was then, that in obedience to a
mandate from her own fair hand, I hoped
to find her in the pavilion of her garden,
fhe having, by reafon of a feigned indifpofition, propofed to the Thane to fleep alone
in a feparate apartment.   The reft, my
dear friend, you know ; and thence you
may judge how unhappy I feel myfelf, for
fear of my charmer's reputation.'

' I expreffed the moft perfect fenfibility
of the confidence with which *Macbeth* had
honoured me ; bid him hope for every fervice I could do for him, in difappointing
the confequences of what he feared ; and,
as the beft return I could make him for
that truft he had repofed in me, I told him
he fhould immediately be the confidant to
an affair of mine, of the fame nature, and
to me equally interefting.   I then communicated to him, that *Jaquenetta*, the beautiful fifter of his beloved *Anabella*, was no
lefs the object of my adoration than *Anabella* was of his ! That I was not lefs happy
than he in the moft favourable returns for
my

my love; with this difference, that my intriguing meeting with no other obſtructions
than ſuch as decency render neceſſary, my
appetite was not whetted by the ſame ſort
of difficulties which gave a reliſh to his,
but which however, to one of my more
ſedate diſpoſition, does by no means leſſen
the enjoyment.——You know (I ſaid) the
two factions, which pretend to divide the
court; thoſe of *Caithneſs* and of *Roſs*.
Gaury, the huſband of my engaging *Jaquenetta*, is wholly in the intereſt of *Roſs*,
from whoſe favour with the king he pro-
miſes himſelf no little influence: ambition
is his chief aim, to that he ſacrifices every
other conſideration, and makes him uncommonly anxious to engage all the young
noblemen he can, to eſpouſe the faction of
Roſs; and carefully adapts his baits to the
inclinations of the party he would proſelyte;
and as youth is for the moſt part in purſuit
of pleaſures, under the influence of ſome
one predominant paſſion; one he entertains
with muſic; to another he covers his table
with the moſt coſtly repaſts; a third he will
mount upon the fineſt horſe of his ſtables;
and amongſt ſome, he will even diſſipate his
money at play. He was not long of diſ-
covering, that the bent of my inclinations
leaned another way, and from a ſteady application to my looks, he ſoon read from

E 3

my eyes, that the fair *Jaquenetta* was the deareſt object of my ſoul :—the diſcovery gave him more joy than diſturbance ; he was happy to think, that he had in his power a bribe, that might engage me to abandon a party he imagined I was before inclined to : invitations to his houſe became more than uſually frequent ; he careſſed me with the affections of a brother, and aſſured me of ſuch a preference in his eſteem, that he would conſtantly employ all his power to ſerve me. After dinner, he would artfully contrive ſuch amuſements for the reſt of his company, as beſt ſuited their reſpective palates, that he might give me the better opportunities of offering my addreſſes to his wife ; and leave her to im-prove upon the leſſon ſhe had got from him to ſollicit my inclinations in favour of the Thane of *Roſs*. Such a ſollicitreſs, you may be ſure, could not, to one of my complexion, and who was truly enamoured paſſionately with her perſon, urge a ſuit in vain. It is true, that on purpoſe to enhance the value of the condeſcenſion I intended to pay her, I repreſented my attachments for the houſe of *Caithneſs* to be much deeper founded than in fact they ever had been ; for if the truth had been known, the ſacrifice I was to make her was but little worth the courting, ſince, in my private

opinion,

opinion, neither of the contending parties
merited the approbation of any man of
confequence; and I affured myfelf, that it
could not be a long while before fome
other, as powerful, and more deferving
than either of them, would fupercede them
both : however, if I had before made my
election upon neither of the fides, the
powerful applications of *Jaquenetta* now
certainly determined me, but not without
perfuading her, that the arguments of her
eyes, which were ten thoufand times more
irrefiftible than every other plea that could
be urged in favour of the Thane of *Rofs*,
had alone commanded my inclinations, as
effectually as her matchlefs charms had captivated my heart.——It was with joy I perceived that the tendernefs with which I
poured forth my fentiments for her, was
not difregarded ; and although, in the beginning, fhe conducted herfelf with a decorum which forbid the moft diftant approaches of any thing indelicate, yet, by
the almoft daily opportunities with which
her good-natured Thane furnifhed me of
enforcing my fuit, I had the fatisfaction to
find that I gained fome ground in every
interview; in fo much, that after the third
or fourth ferious conference, the expreffions
of my paffion grew warmer and warmer,
and were liftened to without that repugnance

nance with which she checked them in the
beginning of our acquaintance. I dared, now,
to approach her lovely person, to grasp her
trembling hand, and ravish an intoxicating
kiss, without affronting her. Upon these,
and such like introductory advances, resistance on her part became weaker, as passion
on my side gathered greater force, and
hurried on to unrepulsed liberties, which
filled my every nerve with vast emotion!
On one tempting occasion, pressing her to
my glowing bosom, I could perceive, from
the enchanting movement of her's, that love
was pleading as successfully for me as she had
follicited for *Rofs!* With my moistened lips
glued to her snowy neck, I smothered opposition, and sucked consent to joy!—She
sunk in my embrace!—I vowed eternal
fidelity and love! and profiting of the
lucky minute, revelled in those sweets
which bounteous nature has provided to
make life worthy mankind's care!———
This, the first scene of our felicity, being
happily closed, the charmer gently reproved
me for having catched an advantage over
her weakness; saying, that although the
power of resistance had been disarmed by
so warm applications, yet her heart entirely disapproved of her folly. I soothed
her well affected repentance, by promises,
not only of the most inviolable attachment
which

which the sincerest love and gratitude for
the bliss she had bestowed could ensure,
but I made fresh protestations to her, that
my interest and operations at court should
be totally at her disposal. I pressed her to
name the happy hour, when I might renew
my professions, but too nice a delicacy
would not permit her at that juncture to
satisfy my request; yet, when with a lover's
salute, I took my leave, she dismissed me
with a smile that was not unpromising.
In conformity to my engagement, I the
very next court day openly associated
with *Ross*'s party, to the no small surprize
of many nobles, who had long laboured in
vain to procure a declaration from me.
You yourself, I believe, wondered at it;
and to this hour, the cause of so sudden an
effect is only known to *Jaquenetta*, her
husband, to love, and now to *Macbeth!*
For as courtly strife is by no sort of means
actuated by motives of public good, but is
merely a contention for power, for places,
and for the king's ear; I look'd at the parties until that moment with such an indifferent eye, that a much less cogent argument than the inestimable love of *Jaquenetta*
would have swayed me to either side.———
And now, my dear *Macbeth*, in return of
yours, you are now the only confident in
the amour of your charming *Anabella*'s
sister---

fifter—And fuperlatively happy I am, replied *Macbeth*, in fuch an interesting confidence.—It looks as if our fouls were, by
fo fympathetic a connection, deftined to
an intimacy, which I fhall ftudy to improve
to our mutual advantage. We exchanged
vows of unalterable friendfhip for one another, the firft proof of which fell to my
fhare, by an anxious appearance at court,
to learn what had become of the young
Caithnefs, and what animadverfions had
been made upon the fubject of his wounds.
I was earlier than ordinary, and yet the
Thane of *Caithnefs* had got the ftart of me.
With unufual fury in his countenance, he
accofted me, as he propofed to do by every
nobleman that entered, and endeavoured
to prepoffefs me againft *Macbeth*, by greatly aggravating every circumftance of the
affault, an unmanly one, as he termed it,
upon his fon. He remonftrated, That if
fuch exceffes were permitted to go unpu-
nifhed, even with Princes of the blood,
none of the nobility fhould be fafe, in attempting to oppofe them in the perpetration of the moft unjuftifiable outrages.—
That *Macbeth*'s affault upon the life of his
fon had no other provocation, than that
Thurfo, feeing three innocent gentlemen
overpowered by numbers of bravadoes,
who attended to fupport *Macbeth* in fome
fecret

ſecret and deſperate enterprize ; he bravely joined himſelf to the weakeſt ſide, and fell a ſacrifice to his generoſity : That theſe gentlemen had been remarkably the objects of *Macbeth*'s reſentment, he having before got them diſmiſſed from profitable places, to make room for ſome of his own creatures ; and that next he purpoſed to ſend them out of the world ; for that one of them, an old gentleman, had actually fallen in defence of his ſon, who was hardly puſhed by ſome of *Macbeth*'s deſperadoes ! In this manner did old *Caithneſs* very forcibly repreſent his ſon's caſe, and ſupplicated every nobleman to ſurround the king, how ſoon he ſhould enter the audiencechamber, and demand the Royal Juſtice upon ſuch a flagitious aſſaſſination !——Although *Caithneſs* was not of the blood royal, he was a powerful man in his own country, by which he had gained ſuch an intereſt with the king, that could he have carried this well-framed tale into belief, and in fact it made impreſſion upon many, it muſt have gone hard with *Macbeth*, then but young at court, and not much favoured by the King. *Caithneſs* had obſerved, that his relation was attended to by me rather contemptuouſly than otherwiſe ; he now therefore left me out of the circle of his abettors, and whiſpered amongſt his intimates,

mates, that he feared this outrage, barbarous as it was, would be palliated by all
the faction of the Thane of *Rofs* ; although
Rofs himfelf, who by this time had joined
the courtiers, and giving credit to the af-
fertions of his rival *Caithnefs*, was one of
the foremoft to condemn *Macbeth*. The
King being entered, the old Thane of
Caithnefs, with tears in his eyes, and fupported by a train of followers, fell on his
knees before the King, briefly recounted
the tragical ftory of the affault; and fuppli-
cated juftice for the lofs of a noble fon,
who then lay expiring with the wounds he
had received from a band of ruffians headed
by *Macbeth*. His complaint was feconded,
not only by all his own, but by many of
the *Rofs* faction ; and the enraged *Duncan*
was ready to pronounce an order for the
immediate fecuring of *Macbeth*, until the
event of *Thurfoe*'s life or death fhould con-
ftitute the criminality of the action ; when
I interpofed, and humbly. prayed his Majefty's attention for a moment; and having
his permiffion to fpeak, I briefly, but with
firmnefs, told him, ' That, to my certain
knowledge, the old Thane himfelf had
been grofsly impofed upon, and that now
he had endeavoured alfo to impofe upon
his King: That no perfon then prefent,
but myfelf, was capable of putting the true
light

light upon that affair, which I said was indeed a horrid one, but horrid on the part
of *Thurfoe*, not on the part of *Macbeth!*
who, but for my accidental intervention,
muft have been bafely butchered by vile
affaffins hounded upon him by the cowardly
Thurfoe. I expreffed my forrow for the
father's tears, but I could not mention the
bafenefs of the fon, fo well known to me,
in milder words,---That three daftardly
villains had been employed by him to maf-
facre *Macbeth!* for what reafon, was beft
known to his own guilty confcience! That
luckily for your Majefty's kinfman, the
noble *Macbeth*, I paffed that way, and faw
him, then unknown to me, defending himfelf, with his fingle arm, againft the united
fury of three! The laws of humanity engaged me to affift the weakeft; and ani-
mated by my arrival, he pufhed his adverfaries with redoubled force, and inftantly
laid one of them fprawling at his feet.
The other two daftards fought to efcape,
but were interrupted by their mafter *Thurfoe*, who till then lay in ambufh waiting the
event. He reproached them with cow-
ardice, and led them back himfelf to renew
the affault; when *Macbeth* inftantly propofed, that as his quarrel was only with
him, they fhould fingly decide it. *Thurfoe*, thus provoked to fair combat, unwilling

as

as he might be to accept it, could not well refuse the honourable challenge, the rather, that his emissaries shewed no great inclination to run any farther risk with him.--- *Macbeth* sustained the first onset from *Thursoe*, and the wounds he received, tho' not dangerous, confine him, nevertheless, at this moment, to his chamber: but after two or three turns, it was the fate of *Thursoe* to yield to the braver arm of his more honourable antagonist. This, my Royal Master, is the true account of the falsified relation you have heard. I hope I need not appeal to the evidence of two villains in support of the testimony I have given; and yet, if *Caithness* should discredit mine, I am convinced that they durst not, in the Royal Presence, contradict the fact, as I have told it.'

' The good King was at once moved with indignation against the son, whilst he could not help compassionating the deluded father, who flunk, confounded, from the Royal Presence.'

' The heads of the *Ross* faction being by, triumphed in this affront upon their rival's family, and courted every opportunity of engaging *Macbeth* to be of their party. They espoused his cause with great warmth, not so much in honour of himself, as to throw the more dishonour upon the interest

of

of their adverfaries, which from that hour began to decline, and as faft did *Macbeth's* reputation and his power begin to rife :— and from thence indeed may be dated the commencement of all thofe honours he afterwards acquired, as well as that fatal ambition, which grew with power to tyranny, and, in all probability, from tyranny to ruin!

' The *Roffians*, that they might the better avail themfelves of this advantage gained over their adverfaries, and that they might the better confirm *Macbeth* in their intereft, petitioned the King, that a day might be appointed for an inquiry into that dark affair, to the end that *Macbeth*, if innocent, fhould get a fair opportunity of clearing himfelf from the ungenerous afperfions imputed to him; and on the other hand, that the young *Caithnefs* fhould be brought to legal trial for fo daring and criminal an affault upon the perfon of one of the Royal blood! The King could not but comply with fo plaufible a demand for juftice, and accordingly fixed the hearing for the tenth day after the phyficians fhould pronounce the life of *Thurfoe* to be out of danger.'

' The noble *Banquho*, alfo one of the Blood-royal, and coufin to *Macbeth*, was amongft the foremoft who vehemently

called

called for juftice againft the *Caithnefs* family; urging, That as the old Thane, whilft he imagined that his fon was the injured party, infifted, that even the Royal blood of *Macbeth* fhould not fcreen him from punifhment; fo it was certainly reafonable, that Juftice fhould, now that the tables were turned, ftand forth for him, as well as againft him; for, otherwife, fuch factious nobility might, in the next place, be tempted to promote their ambitious purpofes, by affaulting the Throne itfelf!'

'The *Caithnefs* faction had many confultations about this knotty affair, which threatened more mifchief to their party than any thing that had hitherto befallen them. The Thane himfelf was a man of confummate fkill, gave much application, and had great addrefs in public affairs. Withal, he was extremely generous; fo that in the general, his fchemes were well laid, and promifed fuccefs, if they had not been, for the moft part, defeated by an impatience and impetuofity of temper, which he could not command, and which was fo well known to his enemies, that they feldom failed to make their account of it, when his fchemes came to be debated in council. The Thane of *Rofs*, his competitor, was a man of a clear head, and fo cool and fedate in debate, that it was not

in

in the power of man to ruffle his temper, or make him deviate from that moderation, by which he uniformly fteered his actions: but then he was avaritious and refentful; there was no meafure to his ambition, nor bounds to his luft for wealth; although he could judge well, who fhould, and who fhould not, participate of the public fpoils. Their partifans were feafoned, more or lefs, with the different qualities of their leaders. Thofe of *Caithnefs* were generally hot-headed, but generous; and thofe of *Rofs* affable and courteous, but rapacious and niggardly."

' The King was weak and indolent, and had not capacity to convert the different talents of thefe rivals to the public fervice. Now the one, then the other, was uppermoft; and the kingdom expofed to be the fpoil of any invader who might have addrefs enough to engage the outed party in his intereft; by which means the people in general were kept in conftant inquietude.'

' In one of the debates of the *Caithnefs* faction, it was refolved, that *Thurfoe*, fo foon as he fhould be able, fhould communicate to the Thane of *Kyle* the intrigue between his wife and *Macbeth*, and endeavour to perfuade him, that the wounds and difgrace he had fuffered, were entirely owing to his zeal for the honour of *Kyle's* family.

family. This rash resolution was but too agreeable to the hot temper of the young *Caithness*, he hoping thereby not only to revenge himself on the lady's partiality and neglect of him, but to excite such a jealousy into *Kyle*, as should rouse his revenge against the man who had wronged his bed and honour, to such a height, as might induce him to put some plot in execution, to destroy the author, and thereby defeat the force of what he was afraid should come out against him at the appointed trial : And lastly, that it would probably carry over *Kyle* to the *Caithness* interest, when he should be convinced that the spoiler of his honour was himself not only attached to the *Rossian* party, but in this case supported with all their power.---*Thurso* therefore, without waiting a perfect recovery, sent a message to the Thane of *Kyle*, intimating an intention to wait upon him the following morning, having business of the last importance to his reputation and honour to communicate. An affair which had made so much noise at court, could now be a secret to no body, and every one had from curiosity been inquisitive into the first cause of the rencounter. Amongst others, *Kyle* himself had heard whispers, which could not be very agreeable to him ; and although his
lady

lady had employed every addreſs to ſmother his awakened ſuſpicions, and that it was not now accounted very creditable to be in any ſort of connections with the young *Caithneſs*; yet that natural anxiety, which is ever the concomitant of jealouſy, very much diſpoſed the unſatisfied *Kyle* to admit of *Thurſoe*'s viſit. *Anabella* happened to be with her Thane when the meſſage was delivered; and although ſhe ſhrewdly ſuſpected what was to be the purport of it, yet her prudence directed her not to interfere in the anſwer, nor to appear to be in the leaſt affected with the meſſage: on the contrary, ſhe aſſumed an unuſual gaiety, and by every poſſible artifice, laboured to prepoſſeſs her huſband with the moſt favourable opinion of her fidelity. In the mean while, ſhe was not without the moſt uneaſy cogitations: ſhe could not doubt, but the incenſed *Thurſoe*, from reſentment of ſlights from her, and the diſgrace he had ſuffered by the hand of *Macbeth*, would provoke him to do them both every miſchief his envenomed mind could contrive; but ſtill ſhe flattered herſelf, that unleſs he had corrupted her maid, who was ſingly in the ſecret of the aſſignation in queſtion, he could not ſuſtain any allegations againſt her, with the ſmalleſt degree of evidence. She was unwilling to tax

her

her confidante with such an ugly suspicion
of her fidelity; and yet, the more she
thought on every circumstance, the more
her doubts increased: she could not conceive what should have brought the assassins
so precisely to the spot of assignation, if
they had not been well directed to it; and
as no other person but her maid could give
such a direction, she at last determined to
question her about it. She did so; and as
it is repugnant to the nature of the meanest
of human kind to confess the guilt of
treachery, the maid endeavoured rather to
evade than absolutely to deny the charge;
which confirmed her mistress that she had
been betrayed, and that the consequence
would be her ruin. However, as it was
the wisest course rather to expostulate with
than to reproach her upon that occasion,
she played her cards so well, that, with
tears of repentance, the maid confessed her
fault; owned, that the bribes of *Thurfoe*
were too valuable to be resisted; that she
did not foresee the fatal consequences it had
been attended with; but, in fine, she prayed
for her mistress's forgiveness; begged that
she would not give way to such despondency, for she would exert all her skill,
and did not doubt of succeeding, yet, to
turn the cannon against the ungenerous
Thurfoe. The night, however, proved a
very

very reftlefs one to the fearful *Anabella!*
Her peace, her reputation, were at ftake,
and with thefe, the credit and rifing glory
of the only man on earth fhe truly loved!
The morning came, and to a moment of
the appointed hour, *Thurfoe* found his way
to *Kyle*'s apartment. They had not been
many minutes together, before the maid is
fummoned to attend : fhe inftantly obeyed,
and the ftill doubting *Anabella* flipt into an
adjoining room, there to liften to what
fhould pafs, and to determine, from what
fhe might hear, whether to abide, or to
fly from, the confequence. *Bella* (for fo
the maid was called) entered the room with
great compofure. The Thane prepared
her for the importance of the affair: he
told her, that he had always regarded her
as a girl of great veracity ; that a family
affair, more interefting to him than life
itfelf, was now the fubject of deliberation ;
that it totally depended upon her teftimo-
ny to obviate every remaining doubt : He
defired her to hear attentively what the
young Lord *Caithnefs* had to fay to her,
and, without fear or favour of any mortal,
to be diftinct and ingenuous in her anfwers,
and that fhe might truft to his well known
liberality for the reward of her honefty.—
The Thane having done, *Thurfoe* next
addreffed himfelf, to this purpofe : ——
" The

" The discovery, my dear Bella, which you made to me some weeks ago, of your lady's intrigue with Macbeth, has lain so heavy on my conscience, that I could not rest until I had acquainted my honoured friend with the seduction of his wife, and the dishonour of his bed, by the treachery of that worthless man !—The lady of Kyle is indeed a tempting object ; in the beauties of person, she's an angel ! What pity it is, that she was not also heavenly in her mind and manners ? It is you, my faithful girl, that can best farther inform the noble Thane with what truths, touching his lady's infidelity, it now so much concerns him to know."

The maid, without the least symptom of fear, or change of countenance, resentfully replied, " Surely, Sir, you are mad, and know not what you say ! Is it like a man of noble blood, by such base and ungenerous aspersions, to revenge your slighted love, by accusing the virtuous Anabella of being guilty with another, because she detested you ? What injustice is it to deny to her other beauties, that firmness of mind, of which you have had such full experience, by her preferring the settled and sincere affections of her aged Lord, to the less solid, but vicious addresses of a debauched youth ? Is this a generous return for her

uncommon,

uncommon, tho' prudential, goodnefs, in
not expofing you to the juft refentment of
her injured Thane? Oh! how it provokes
me to think you could imagine, that this
ring, with fome other paultry prefents
which you made me, was intended to bribe
me, either to betray my lady's honour, or
accufe her of a crime her foul abhors!"—
The exafperated *Thurfoe* could hold no
longer, but vehemently interrupted her
with,—" Thou monfter of a woman! is it
poffible that fo much impudence and guilt
can meet in one perfon? Was it not you
who informed me of the affignation, on the
fatal night which brought me to difappoint
Macbeth, and fave the honour of my friend?
and had you not my gold for the intelligence?"——" True, Sir, (anfwered fhe)
I had your gold, and will keep it too; but
won't you blufh when I dare tell you, in
prefence of my Lord, that it was given to
entice me to let you enter filently the garden door, becaufe you knew the Thane was
abfent? and becaufe I knew, that if I acted
fuch a foul part, I fhould for ever forfeit
the favour, both of my Lord and Lady, I
tried to put you off the fcent, by telling
you, that *Macbeth*, whom I was fure you
feared and hated, fometimes amufed himfelf in an evening behind thefe walls, with
fome damfels unknown to me; but which

was

was no more than an artifice, whereby without offending my miftrefs, I might fecure your gold."——-Never did artful woman better act her part than now did *Bella*. She not only preferved *Anabella*'s peace and reputation, and confounded the growing jealoufy of the old Thane; but by an adroitnefs peculiar to the well-trained *Abigails*, ingenioufly accounted for *Macbeth*'s being at the time and place when *Thurfoe*'s emiffaries had found him!---*Thurfoe* ftared like one diftracted; and although his breaft was replete with wrath, he could not utter one fyllable! The Thane of *Kyle*, between refentment and aftonifhment, at length as gravely as cuttingly, told him, That thofe prejudices which are natural in favour of a man of noble birth, would have inclined me to give preference to your evidence againft a fervant's, if the probabilities were equal; but as her's is fupported by argument and good nature, whilft your's feems to have no other foundation but revenge and malevolence, I muft undoubtedly reject it, and defpife you for an injurious attempt to rob my faithful *Anabella* of her fame, and me of my happinefs, for no other reafon, than becaufe fhe refufed to facrifice her virtue to your infidious and criminal addreffes! Avaunt! be gone! infamous wretch! It is well for thee, that
thy

thy well-deserved wounds, not yet healed,
protect thee from that chastisement which
should be the due of so much audacity!---
So saying, he left him overwhelmed in
agonies of confusion, giving orders to a
servant to shew him out of his gates.

'The re-animated *Anabella*, who had been
an ear-witness of all that passed, met her
artful *Abigail* with a thousand caresses;
and immediately proceeding to the audi-
ence-chamber, she saluted her Thane with
unaffected gaiety, not inclining to leave
him too long alone, left his revolving
the several circumstances seriously in his
mind, might, notwithstanding *Bella*'s well
calculated evidence, leave some unfavourable impressions; which, in fact, happened
to be the case : for although he could not
directly condemn his wife, yet he now began to compare, with more exactitude than
formerly, the youth, the bloom, the manly
shape, the vigour, and, to sum up all, the
flourishing prospect of *Macbeth*'s situation,
opposed to the impotencies of age in every
one of these regards; the consequence of
which was, that he subjected himself to the
alarms of perpetual suspicion ; and became
so much the more and more watchful over
every motion of *Anabella*, that he rendered
her life very irksome to her, and the stolen

G   enjoyments.

enjoyments of her paramour were now obtained at a moſt imminent riſk to both.

'Delights, which are thus purſued contrary to decency, to reaſon, to religion, and to every rule of hoſpitality, are ſeldom permanent, and ſeldom terminate without the mark of ſome fatal cataſtrophe : ſo it was with this libidinous couple ; for having now no opportunity of gratifying their looſe deſires within doors, they reſorted to a private corner in one of the gardens. *Macbeth* found means to ſcale the wall from without, whilſt *Anabella* gave him the meeting from within ; and as their ſolacements were, for the moſt part, nocturnal, it happened, during one of their private interviews, that the old Thane being reſtleſs, miſſed his wife, and without calling up any ſervant, went in ſearch of her : he thought of the garden, into which there being a paſſage through a glaſs door from the bathing-room, by a ſlight moveable ſtair-caſe, which, upon thoſe occaſional meetings, the cautious *Anabella* took care ſhould always be removed, for fear of ſurprize : the unwary Thane not dreaming of ſuch a precipitate Ha, ha, ſought that inlet to the garden, and tumbled headlong into it ; there he lay motionleſs, until *Anabella* returning from her pleaſures, was alarmed by the grumbling ſound of laſt groans ! She re-entered the houſe by

by another door, of which fhe kept the key ;
fhe awaked her trufty *Bella*, but upon difclofing her fufpicion of the fatal accident, the
maid, warm as fhe was in the intereft of
the lovers, was fo immenfely fhocked, that
fhe fhrieked aloud, and very much hazarded
a difcovery of the whole ! But the miftrefs,
though alfo very much affected, had more
command of herfelf, and urging their mutual fafety to be the ftake, fhe reafoned her
maid into compofure. They next con-
fulted, as to what was fitteft to be done in
fuch a critical circumftance : they went into the garden, and found the unfortunate
Thane, with his neck diflocated, juft expired ! They removed again the occafional
ftair-cafe, and placing part of it acrofs
the Thane's body, and by the help of an
iron bolt, diftorting one of the fixing hooks,
endeavoured to give the whole an appearance of accident. The maid next returned
to her bed, whilft *Anabella* rung feveral
times her bell. At length another maid
got up, and coming to the lady's apartment, fhe was ordered to get a light, and
to awake *Bella*, and at the fame time afked
if fhe had feen or heard any thing of the
Thane ? *Bella* was now ordered to attend
her miftrefs ; and candles being got, all the
three fearched over the houfe for their mafter, until arriving at the bathing-room,

they

they found the door into the garden unfolded; and *Anabella* obferving that the steps were gone, affected a woeful fhriek. They returned immediately, and then paffed into the garden by the ordinary door; and coming into the walk under the bathing-room windows, they found the dead body of the Thane! The real lamentations of the ignorant fervant, and the well diffembled grief of *Anabella*, and her other maid, gave the whole every appearance of chance. The men fervants were now fummoned up, and the Thane's body tranfported immediately into his chamber. Thus was the unhappy death of *Kyle*, which was truly the confequence of his wife's unlawful wantonnefs, impofed upon the world, as merely the effect of unlucky accident. For fome days, however, fhe obferved, with the greateft ftrictnefs, that forrowful decorum, which is often diffembled, although fometimes real, ufually paid to the *manes* of a deceafed hufband; but the ftill enamoured *Macbeth* prevented, by his now lefs interrupted vifits, the effects from piercing her heart too deeply.

'This intrigue, like moft others of the fame condemnable nature, began, however, fooner than *Anabella* wifhed or expected, to draw towards its eve.'

The

The sketches originally written by *Angus*, and now delivered by *Edmund*, terminating here, the Thane himself resumed the narration.

' Self-flattery (continued he) is a natural companion of real love. *Anabella* loved *Macbeth* with uncommon ardour; she believed their passions were reciprocal; and indeed, hitherto, she had not much reason to doubt of it; but thereupon her imagination had formed a structure, which the foundation was never intended to sustain. She was in hopes, there being now no obstacle in the way, that *Macbeth*, in conformity to the many vows he had breathed upon her enchanting bosom, would supply the place of her deceased Thane, not only in one, but in every sense. She hoped to confine him perpetually to her arms; and assuming now more the dignity of a wife than the tameness of a mistress, she would sometimes appear inquisitive into the employment of those hours which were lost to her attention, and chide, if the accounts he gave of himself were not satisfactory. The temper of *Macbeth*, ever repugnant to discipline and restraint, or to any thing that bore the most distant resemblance of either, could by no means brook an attempt to fix by chains those pleasures, which he had

G 3   chaced

chaced with the keener appetite, because
they were purchased with difficulties, and
because he reckoned them unconfined; did
by no means relish the insinuations which
stole from *Anabella*, of her desiring to change
the mode of their amour; besides, as another sort of ambition, which could be but
little forwarded by a lady in *Anabella*'s circumstances, began to occupy no small place
in his active soul, the softer passions sub-
siding, made room for others of a more
elevated nature.'

‘ At this critical juncture, *Margaretta*,
daughter to the Chieftain of *Ross*, made her
appearance at court: she was more graceful than lovely, and studied how she might
rather command than court respect: her
understanding was superior to most of
her cotemporaries; and if she had no great
share of personal delicacy, there were none
of the court ladies that were, however, so
remarkably distinguished for personal dignity: her manner, more than her beauty,
attracted the attention of *Macbeth*, and the
powerful connections of her family disposed
his mind to an alliance which could so effectually cherish his ambition. The lady,
on her part, discovered charms in the manly
deportment of *Macbeth*, which, in his favour, wrought equal impressions in her
aspiring breast. To be short, their dispositions

ctions seemed to be so aptly fitted to one
another, that it was not long ere they mutually communicated their respective appro-
bations; and the lately so delightful Anabella, with all the beauty which symmetry
of features, gentleness of soul, and engaging affability, could make a woman
lovely, was now abandoned by the only
man she had ever sincerely loved, and all to
make room for another lady, greatly inferior
to her in almost every attraction which
usually captivates, and often secures the
admiration of mankind. Think of Anabella, ye fair charmers, whenever your
virtue is besieged by deluding men!—to
whose seducing wiles you are so often in-
veigled to sell, with your virtue, all that
peace of mind which can best support you
through every vicissitude of life, and by the
loss of which you subject yourselves to be
slighted by those very paramours, to
whose pleasures your every faculty have
been exerted.'

' Macbeth was now under a necessity of
directing his addresses in a manner entirely
new to him; the formal advances towards
the matrimonial point must guide his conduct. It is true, he had almost no difficulties to surmount; the desires of both the
parties were influenced more by ambition,
and a thirst for dominion, than by love.
The

The active mind of *Macbeth* was ever foaring beyond the limits of his prefent condition ; and he began to fancy, that by being fo clofely linked with the moft powerful, as well as moft popular party, a paffage would open to him, through which he might gain even a profpect of the Crown. The Lady's foul kept pace with his in every afpiring imagination ; and the birth, the fortune, and, above all, the perfonal endowments of *Macbeth*, were too confpicuous, not to make his applications welcome with the Thane of *Rofs* : fo that this match was hardly fooner propofed, than chearfully agreed upon, and a day for the celebration fixed.

' In confequence of this matrimonial treaty, the affair of the young *Caithnefs* was refumed with redoubled ardour, and all the addrefs of his father could not any longer obtain a delay of trial ; but, how foon the day was appointed for it, and known to every body, the now flighted Dowager of *Kyle* fent fuch a meffage to *Macbeth*, as fhook all his refolution ; fhe threatened, at the expence of her own fame, to appear, with her maid, and give fuch a turn to the face of that bufinefs, as fhould greatly embarrafs the profecuting party, caft no fmall degree of blame upon *Macbeth*, and, at leaft, extenuate the guilt of *Thurfoe*. This meffage
did

did not a little perplex our hero; and to prevent any bad effects of it, he judged it highly expedient to renew his visits to the fair, enraged *Anabella*: he had admittance, but was received with such severe, just, and well-seasoned reproach, as greatly disconcerted him: he trusted so entirely to the passionate feelings he knew *Anabella* to entertain for him, that he thought he had only to revive in her, by his presence and caresses, those flames which he flattered himself were yet unextinguished, and thereby lay asleep all her menaced resentment; but *Anabella* had so well fortified herself against the force of his expected artillery, that the task was much more difficult than he imagined. In vain did he renew professions of love, and even of fidelity: she continued, in appearance, unmoved, and treated his advances to embrace her with that disdain which they deserved. A newly assumed determinedness and dignity which she put on upon that occasion, so different from what he conceived her gentle disposition to be capable of, as if she had been a new object, actually inspired him with a new passion for her, and made him wish for the moment that she had been daughter to the Thane of *Rofs*. This new-raised flame of his was not unperceived by *Anabella*; and those well experienced emotions which

which now fhook every nerve of him, became more prevalent over the refolution of
the ftill enamoured charmer, than millions
of verbal affeverations. In fhort, he fucceeded to his wifhes, and once more feafted
in tranfports, which ¡he had never known
fo completely in the embraees of another.
The amorous treaty being over, and *Anabella* thereby better difpofed to liften to
foothing argumentation, he endeavoured to
perfuade her, that he truly loved none but
her ; that the late diftance he had obferved
towards her, was an unwilling facrifice he
had made to the fufpicions of *Margaretta* ;
that his addreffes at that quarter were
merely political, and not from inclination ;
that his future views were founded in them,
and could not be fupported without the
concurrence of that family. He talked
flightly and contemptibly of matrimony, as
an unneceffary confirmation of what was,
by inclination, more folemnly imprinted in
their inmoft fouls : that it was refpect for
her reputation which prevented his ever
hearkening to marriage propofitions with
her, as it would have furnifhed a handle to
their enemies to magnify the fufpicions
which had been already propagated by the
favourers of *Caithnefs* ; and, in fine, that
although his name and politics were to be
united by matrimony in the family of *Rofs*,
he

He vowed that his heart fhould continue un-
alterably devoted to his charming *Anabella*.
The ftrong impreffions which thofe endear-
ments fo recently renewed between them,
operated fo effectually upon the credu-
lous mind of *Anabella*, that fhe fwallowed
all this fophiftry with approbation, and
gained her over to a thorough reconcile-
ment. *Macbeth* was happy in his fuccefs,
and for once more took his leave of her
with a cordial affection.

  ' There remaining now no obftruction
to the profecution of *Thurfoe*, the trial was
brought on ; a pardon was obtained for the
villains he had employed in the affaffination ; and by their evidence corroborating
mine, he was convicted of the bafe crime
imputed to him ; he was fentenced to lofe
his head. But the artful *Macbeth*, anxious
to found his rife on popularity, as well as
power, interceded himfelf, that the judgment might be converted from death to banifhment : he eafily obtained his fuit ; and
in conformity thereto, the unfortunate
Thurfoe was condemned to depart for the
Ifles within a fortnight, and there to remain
an exile during the King's pleafure.

  ' Amongft the partifans of *Caithnefs*,
there was one *Macduald*, who had a vaft
influence in the Ifles, was of an enterprizing genius, and being difgufted by neglect,
                                   had

had conceived a settled antipathy against
Macbeth. Many of the *Caithness* faction
gave *Thurso* the convoy of a day's journey;
but this *Macdnald*, with some of his followers, proposed to accompany him quite
to the place of exile, intending, with the
son of the lately revered *Caithness* at their
head, to stir up the Islanders, who were of
themselves very formidable, to commotion;
and by their means, and such a junction as
might be hoped for from amongst the other
malecontents, to create such a disturbance
as might enable him to gratify his revenge,
not against *Macbeth* and his party only, but
against the King himself, as we shall see by
and by.

'In the mean time, preparations were
going forward to solemnize, with every
magnificence, the marriage of *Macbeth*,
which was celebrated in presence of the
King, and a most splendid court. Soon
after which, the Thane of *Caithness* seeing
no sort of hope of regaining either respect
or interest at court, bethought him of ex-
erting his abilities upon some other plan.
He was possessed of a very extensive and
well peopled estate in the North; and the
Thanes of *Nairn* and *Sutherland*, whose
properties lay not very distant from his,
and who were also the superiors of a people
as turbulent as they were potent, who had
closely

closely adhered to him in all his minifterial meafures, and who now fhared in his difgrace ; thefe Chieftains he infpired with the like difcontents which preyed upon himfelf : them he perfuaded to forfake the Lowlands, and to accompany him to the North, that they might firft found, and then try to enflame the minds of their refpective clans ; and, according to the encouragement they fhould meet with, and the ftrength they could mufter, to form a project of revenging themfelves upon their enemies. Thefe three Thanes fet out accordingly, attended by a numerous retinue of their dependants.

‘ Mean while, the bufy *Macduald*, carrying in his hand the banifhed *Thurfoe* through the weftern iflands, produced him amongft thefe people, as a diftinguifhed mark of thofe defpotic and tyrannical meafures, under which he faid the greateft part of *Scotland* was then groaning ; and making them believe, that unlefs a timely and ftrenuous oppofition was formed, oppreffion, mifery and maffacres, would very foon be extended as far as the Ifles, when it fhould be paft their power to help themfelves. Thefe feditious meafures had a wonderful effect ; thefe uninformed people, like the lowermoft clafs of every other country, have ears always more open to

fcandal

scandal than to encomiums, upon the actions of their betters; and a malignant emissary will ever find it an easier task to promote disturbance and insurrection, by the means of calumny, and abuse of those in power, than a benevolent agent will find it, to dispose the same rank of men to stand forth in defence of a conduct the most laudable. Men of bad hearts can, with more facility, disguise themselves, than men of upright, incorruptible principles : *These* wish to sustain an uniformity of character, and therefore cannot descend to huzza with a misguided multitude; whilst *Those*, having no dignity to support, nor reputation to lose, can level themselves with the meanest of a mob, to gain numbers to their faction. In this shape it was that *Macduald* was so extremely successful: the cry of the Islanders was now, No *Ross!* no *Macbeth!*—and, at length, No King!—*Macduald* and Liberty for ever! *Macduald* having thus completely fitted the most turbulent of his people for rebellion, their numbers increased every day, many conjoining to them, not from any real approbation of the motives, but from regard to their own lives and properties; for the insurgents having no controul in these parts, and having usurped the princely authority, there was no safety but in mixing with them;

them; and by that means, (which will for ever be the consequence of lawless commotion) abundance of people suffered in the end, who had been induced by terror, not by inclination, to join themselves to the rebellious standard;

' The Court got intelligence of these outrageous motions, and of the descent which the insurgents were preparing to make into the main land; *Macbeth* and *Bancho* were therefore chosen immediately to lead an army of the best troops of the kingdom to give the insurgents a check; and, if possible, to prevent their being joined by the partisans of *Caithness*, *Nairn* and *Sutherland*, who by this time had also procured a considerable force; and could they have effected a conjunction, their united strength might have become very troublesome.

' The divisions commanded by *Macbeth* and *Bancho* rendezvoused at *Inverness*, and found the people in that neighbourhood under the most terrible apprehensions of the threatened descent of the Islanders; but *Macdual* knew too well what he was about, to quit the Isles, before he should get some reason to believe that some part of the *Caithness* force was ready to support his landing; and he had no sort of apprehension henfion that the King's troops would be rifked in the Ifles.

‘ It was concerted between *Macbeth* and *Bancho*, that the latter fhould proceed with 2,500 men, to line the fhore oppofite to *Caithnefs* and *Sutherland*, and thereby interrupt their getting into *Rofs*-fhire; whilft *Macbeth*, with the main army, fhould march towards the Weftern Iflands. He received intelligence, that all the ftrength of the Rebels was to be collected at *Skie*, there to wait until they fhould receive fome news from *Caithnefs*, thereupon to difperfe by different parties, and to land at once in fo many different places, as to prevent the army from fixing its attention to any one fpot, till it fhould be proper for them to re-affemble, and to form into one body, with their allies from *Caithnefs* and *Sutherland*, who, they thought, would have little difficulty to make good their landing.

‘ *Macbeth* could guefs pretty nearly at the numbers of the Iflanders; he knew he was more completely armed than they could be, and imagined, if he could falute them with a vifit of furprife, he fhould enjoy an eafy enough conqueft: he therefore collected together all the fea-boats upon the coaft, which, however, were not half fufficient for his embarkation: he waited for a favourable evening, and intrepidly ventured
himfelf

himfelf to fea with about 1500 of the beft troops, leaving the reft under the command of a kinfman, named *Kymmin*, (a) to follow how foon he could fend back the boats. The paffage was but fhort, and in favourable weather, could be performed in four or five hours. He fet fail about feven in the evening, and managed it fo, that a few boats, which were of the fame fafhion with thofe of the *Skie* boats, fhould firft gain the ifland, to prevent any fpies from being alarmed by their numbers, to make a rummage alongft the fhore, and to fecure every living perfon they fhould meet with, fo as to prevent intelligence. Thefe advanced boats got footing on the ifland before 11 o'clock; they did as they were ordered, and had made, of old men, women and children, about 40 prifoners. About half an hour after, *Macbeth*, with his ftrange fort of fleet, arrived: he debarked his people with the utmoft expedition, and inftantly fent back the boats to the other coaft.

(a) Probably the anceftor of the ancient, and afterwards fo numerous name of *Cumin*, now fubdivided into a variety of different modes of riting it, fuch as *Cummin, Cummyn, Comyns, Cumming*. &c. a conjecture the more natural, that it is faid they retain in *Scotland*, at this day, the pronunciation of that name, as if written *Kymmin*, and not *Cumming*.

They

They continued in a filent and defenfive pofition during the night; and learning from the prifoners that the collected ftrength of the Rebels was near two miles diftant, he hoped his plan would fucceed to his mind. When day-light appeared, he divided his people, and difpofed of them in fo many diftinct confpicuous places, that the enemy might be able to form no certain opinion of their ftrength, or, more properly, of their weaknefs. He faw nothing till towards fix in the morning, that could in the leaft alarm him. About that time feveral fcouting parties were obferved reconnoitring, but quickly difappeared; and by and by he perceived a detached few, feven or eight perfons, advancing near to him: he was fure they could mean no hoftility, and therefore he fhewed a readinefs to welcome them. Thefe were a few of the peaceable people, who had been preffed, contrary to their inclinations, to join the rebellious ftandard: from them he underftood, that *Macduald*'s number amounted to between 3 and 4000, the half of whom, they imagined, would be, like themfelves, glad to abandon the infurgents, if they could find a favourable opportunity. Soon after this, *Macbeth* defcryed the main body of *Macduald*'s party marching along the declivity of a hill, and endeavouring,

as

as he conjectured, to poffefs themfelves of
a very advantageous ground, which they
had but juft gained, when he could alfo
difcover the boats returning with *Kymmin*'s
divifion, within half an hour's fail of the
beach. The fame difcovery had been alfo
made, much about the fame time, by the
enemy, who, in hopes to harrafs them in
their landing, profited of a hill which covered part of his people from the obfervation of *Macbeth*. He ordered about four
hundred of his moft refolute people, under
the command of a very daring kinfman, to
file off by the farther fide of the hill, and
to endeavour, unperceived, to gain the
beach. *Kymmin* defcried their approach,
and guefling at their defign, he hurried the
landing of as many of his men as might be
able to make a diverfion, and cover the
landing of the reft, until he fhould think
himfelf ftrong enough to make an offenfive
attack. This manœuvre he executed with
great prudence, and very little lofs ; and
indeed it was of great confequence ; for
although, with the handful that were landed, he might have given them the flip, and
got within fignals of *Macbeth*, yet he muft
in that cafe have left his empty boats in
their power, and the largeft part of his divifion, ftill unlanded, muft have re-taken
themfelves to fea, and hazarded the effects
of

of a gale of wind, which then feemed to threaten them. His defence was the eafier, that the enemy durft not pufh him beyond a certain limit, for fear of expofing their attempt to the view of *Macbeth*, an advantage which *Kymmin* managed fo well, that while he continued fkirmifhing, the bulk of his command made good their landing, and thereupon the *Macdualds* began to retire. *Kymmin* was under a neceffity of purfuing them, becaufe had he left them, and proceeded towards *Macbeth*, he fhould have left his miniature of a fleet a prey to the enemy. He purfued fo clofe, that the enemy took fhelter in an old fort on a declivity of the hill, which in front was impregnable to the force of arms ufed in thefe days : he therefore endeavoured to gain the back fide of it, which in a fhort time he effected; but this part being fecured by a wall of fuch thicknefs, and although not very high, yet being built in fuch an oblique manner, that there was no fuch thing as climbing it up; and as they had no fort of materials by which they could rafe any kind of counter parapet, he was on the point of communicating his fituation to *Macbeth*, when, in the courfe of his perambulations, he difcovered, between this and another contiguous hill, a very fertile plain, naturally, and almoft untilled overgrown with

the

the plant known by the name Cumin : he
fet his people inftantly to work upon this
field ; they pulled up and bundled into
fheaves great quantities of this plant, by
piling up of which againft the back wall of
the caftle, they formed an eafy afcent, and
by that means *(a)* a fufficient number
mounted upon it, and defcending, fword
in hand, into the body of the fort, charged
fo brifkly the furprifed enemy, that moft of
them were either flaughtered within the
walls, or expofed to no better a fate, when,
by opening the front paffages, they fought
their flight through the parties that were
pofted there. Some ftragglers having, however, efcaped to the main body, and informed *Macduald* of the mifadventure of
that detachment, he was feized with the
utmoft confternation, and by his irregular
and confufed movements, the dilemma he
was brought to was too obvious not to be
perceived by the watchful *Macbeth*, who
was by this time informed by meffengers
from *Kymmin*, of the circumftances which

(a) It is not very abfurd to imagine, with fome
of that name, that the *garbes* in the field of the arms
of *Cumming*, &c. have an allufion to that æra of an-
tiquity, and reprefent rather three fheaves of the
plant Cumin, than three corn fheaves, as commonly
underftood.

had

had fo long retarded their junction; upon which he immediately made a motion, as if to advance againft them with his whole force: this motion, however, he executed with great deliberation, as he intended it only to procure a farther profpect of their increafing confufion, and to give the better opportunity for deferters to come in. *Kymmin* having now joined him, he formed a plan of extending part of his forces alongft the fkirts of the ifland, to prevent the heads of the cabal from efcaping by fea, in cafe they fhould, when hard drove, think of fuch an attempt; whilft he, with about no more than 1000 chofen men, continued to march flowly after the chief body of rebels. This plan had an excellent effect; it cut off all hopes from the Rebels of any reinforcements; it not only prevented all hopes of efcaping, but the detached parties intercepted, for the ufe of his own troops, fuch provifions as *Macduald* had commanded to be brought from the contiguous fmall iflands; and there was an opening every where for the difcontented of the infurgents to join the royal party at pleafure; and in fact, the defertion from the Rebels was fo great, that *Macduald* was not now above 800 ftrong: with thefe, who were chiefly kinfmen, or altogether dependants on himfelf, he judged it in vain to rifk a battle;

and

and *Macbeth* thinking it proper, by this
time, to make the ifignal agreed upon for
the conjunction of all his out-detachments,
Macduald offered to capitulate ; but as
Macbeth would give him no other terms
than to furrender at difcretion ; from the
confequence of which, as he hoped for no
mercy, he betook himfelf, with his friends, to
another old caftle, which was, for thofe days,
indifferently well fortified. In this fortrefs
he defended himfelf with great refolution
for fome days, till feeing at length that it
was to no purpofe any longer to oppofe
fuch fuperior force, he fubmitted to the inftances of his followers, and agreed to furrender ; but with the fame breath by which
he gave orders to open the gates, neither
chufing to afk, nor expecting mercy from
Macbeth, he fell upon his own fword, and
expired before the enemy got poffeffion of
the caftle ; and the young *Caithnefs*, who
had not the refolution of a *Macduald*, fell a
facrifice to the defperation of fome of *Mac-*
duald's kinfmen, who imputed to him the
caufe of all their calamity. Now it was
that *Macbeth* had the firft opportunity of
giving a fign of that cruelty, which, by his
actions fince, appears to have been at all
times the latent poffeffor of his breaft : he
was as immoveable to the pitiable fubmiffion of the conquered, as he ftood obftinate
against

againft the interceffions of *Kymmin*, and many others of the officers, who were for extending fome degree of clemency :· he argued, that they were a ftubborn, feditious people ; that there was no confidence to be put in them ; that they would, upon another occafion, be juft as ready for a revolt as they had been before ; and as the ifland lay fo remote from the inland, they might find fubfequent occafions of being troublefome, when difturbances in other parts fhould make it inconvenient to fend troops to fubdue them. From fuch a manner of reafoning, there was room to conjecture, that at that period he began to found in his own mind the bafe of his future operations, and to preclude, by extirpation, thefe unhappy people from being any interruption to him, when he fhould be in action elfewhere. He began his feverity, by ordering the head of the dead *Macdwald* to be cut off upon a public fcaffold ; and, to be fhort, the whole garrifon were put to death by one means or other. The body of young *Caithnefs*, indeed, he ordered fhould be buried, that he might thereby fhun the imputation of perfonal revenge : and leaving a few of his own kinfmen, of the name of *Macdonald*, to be mafters of the ifland, with injunctions to them to pick and chufe from amongft the women thofe who were

moft

moft agreeable to them, and to tranfport the reft to other places; he prepared to re-embark his army.

‘ During thefe tranfactions in *Skie*, *Banebo* had fubdued, more by treaty than by conqueft, the Chiefs of *Caithnefs*, *Sutherland* and *Nairn*, who having feen all chance cut off of any communication with the *Macdualds*, were very ready to fubmit to any terms which *Bancho* fhould demand; and accordingly, to prevent his farther incurfions upon them, they, at his defire, fent him hoftages, as a fecurity for their inoffenfive conduct during the fpace of twelve months.

‘ *Bancho* waited the arrival of *Macbeth* at *Invernefs*, from whence they both proceeded to the Court, then at *St. Johnftoun*, or *Perth*, and were welcomed with every mark of approbation. They had enjoyed but a few days of congratulation, when a more ferious affair demanded their attention, and required the united wifdom, as well as ftrength, of the whole kingdom, to form an oppofition to. The *Danes* had lately invaded *England*, and, unknown to the Court of *Scotland*, it had been at the fame time concerted, That, to prevent the *Scotch* from affording any affiftance to *England*, the *Norwegians* fhould, about the fame time, make an attempt upon *Scotland*; and the firft notice of their arrival

I

was

was by the appearance of a very formidable
fleet in the *Frith* of *Forth*, under the command of *Sweno* king of *Norway* himself,
and who, without any interruption, had
made good a landing on the coast of *Fife*.
Macbeth, as the most active, and now the
most powerful person about court, was
quickly commissioned to make a tour thro'
the most popular counties, with a general
summons for all degrees of men to attend
the King's standard, in defence of their
country, their families, lives and fortunes :
this service he performed with great expedition and success. In the mean time, the
King, with *Bancho*, were to endeavour,
with what force they could hastily get together, and the reinforcements which came
daily from *Macbeth*, to advance towards
the enemy, and to keep them in play by
skirmishing, in order to gain time. But
the King, who soon tired of action, did
not know exactly the strength of the *Norwegians*, and who placed an unreasonable
confidence in the prowess of his handful of
men, insisted, contrary to the advice of
Bancho, to advance, and hazard an engagement, rather than suffer the enemy to penetrate into the heart of the kingdom, as the
Danes had done in *England*. Accordingly
he gave them battle ; and although *Bancho*,
both by conduct and bravery, distinguished
himself

himfelf as an able commander, yet with
confiderable lofs, but no difhonour, they
were obliged to quit the field, and to make
good a retreat to *Perth.*

' *Macbeth*, in a few days, joined them at
Perth; and if they had not fuffered fo con-
fiderably in their firft rafh attempt, they
might, by this time, have formed a very
different fort of refiftance. The natural
confequence of fuccefs in war never fails to
infpire the conquerors with frefh vigour;
and the *Norwegians*, who now lived on
plenty, and quite recovered of the fatigue
and indifpofition which attended their voy-
age, became ten times more formidable
than they were at their firft landing. *Macbeth*, who had the moft comprehenfive eye
of moft men living, rode out in difguife to
reconnoitre; and judging, from the numbers and fituation of the *Norwegians*, that
with all the force the King yet could collect, it would be very hazardous to rifk a
decifive engagement; and apprehending,
that from the vicinity of the *Caithnefs* and
Sutherland country to *Norway*, in cafe of a
total defeat, that then the vicegerency of
Scotland might fall into the hands of thefe
difcontented Chiefs, he advifed in counc.l
to gain time, by propofing to treat of a
peace. This motion was approved, and
I was named, as the propereft member of

the

the council to be employed in this negotiation; in confequence of which, I fet out, with proper attendants, for the army of the *Norwegians.* A parley being beat, and admittance granted to the prefence of *Sweno*, I counterfeited fuch an air of fubmiffion and defpondency, that *Sweno*, as well as every officer about him, concluded that the conqueft of the *Scots* would be a very eafy affair. I pathetically reprefented to him, how inutile it would be to promote an effufion of blood, fince the *Scots*, confcious of their inequality to the prefent difpute, wanted only to difpofe him to offer them favourable terms of accommodation. He afked me, if the King my mafter had furnifhed me with the fubftance of fuch conditions as he hoped for; I obfequioufly anfwered him, That the King my mafter, too fenfible to his prefent low circumftances, did not prefume to demand, but confided in the generofity of the *Norwegians* to propofe fuch articles as to him might be acceptable. Such humility greatly flattered the *Norwegian* pride; he told me, That he immediately wanted fome liquors for the better refrefhment of his troops; he required, that I fhould inftantly difpatch a meffenger with orders, that his army might that very day be fupplied with as much wine, fpirits and ale, as could poffibly be
fpared.

ſpared from the other; ſaid, he would call a council that afternoon, to deliberate upon ſuch terms as he would tender to the *Scots*, and ſend me home in the evening with a duplicate. I ſeemed happy with the ſucceſs of my negociation, diſpatched immediately a meſſenger to the King, requeſting, that a moment might not be delayed in ſending to the camp of the *Norwegians* the liquors demanded; upon which diſpatches I affixed a certain ſeal, well known to *Macbeth*, and which imported, that ſome unuſual ſtratagem was to be exerted. Perhaps you, my friends and deliverer, with others of ſcrupulous honour, will cenſure this ſuggeſtion, as unjuſt, and not ſtrictly conſiſtent with the fair rules of war; that nicety I did revolve in my own mind, and reconciled myſelf to the difficulty, upon theſe conſiderations; That the enemies were unprovoked invaders; that they had in a hoſtile manner entered the kingdom, in contravention of ſubſiſting treaties; and that having commenced hoſtilities contrary to the law of nations, they had no right to be treated as an open and declared enemy. That if we could ſubdue them by artifice, we ſhould certainly preſerve the lives of many of our own ſubjects; and as the deſign was not to deſtroy, but to render them inactive, we ſhould even have it in our

power

power to fave numbers of theirs. Be this
as it may, *Macbeth* was too quick not to
profit of the hint; he immediately prepared
foporificks, and, to the knowledge of as
few as poffible, he mixed with a proper
quantity of the infufion, every cafk of the
liquors that were to be fent. Toward night
the impatiently expected efcort arrived with
thefe liquors, and the impatient *Norwegians*
fucked in the fleepy draughts with great
intemperance. How foon the liquors were
delivered, tafted and approved, *Sweno*'s
fecretary delivered me his preliminary articles for a treaty; the firft of which being,
that the *Scots* King, with his whole army,
fhould next day march, without any fort of
arms, and deliver themfelves up at the
Norwegian camp, to the mercy of King
Sweno; I need not enter into the reft. I
took my leave, and returned with the efcort to *Perth*. By this time the valiant men
from *Argylefhire*, with the noble Thane at
their head, had arrived, and now the army
of *Duncan* made no inconfiderable figure.
They were already in order of battle, and
waited only for my return, to proceed in
three divifions, commanded by *Macbeth*,
Bancho and *Argyle*, fo as to affault the
enemy before day-light next morning.
The opiate had had fo fully its effect, that
Macbeth's divifion was in the heart of the
enemy,

enemy, and had made a terrible slaughter before two-thirds of them were awaked to their danger. Happily for *Sweno*, there had been some few near his person, who never drinking strong liquors, were enough in their senses to throw him, intoxicated as he was, across a horse, and hurry off with him towards the sea-side, and had just time to get him and themselves on board a small vessel, before a detachment sent after them could overtake them. The rest of this sleepy army became an easy prey; and it grieves my soul to relate the dreadful effusion of blood which attended this victory; for *Macbeth*, *Bancho*, and almost every Chief, concurring in opinion, that *Canutus*, King of the *Danes*, who was next neighbour, and in strict alliance with *Sweno*, would, as soon as the affairs between him and the *English* should be adjusted, endeavour next to revenge the affront given to *Sweno*, by another attempt upon *Scotland*; the Chiefs, I say, all agreed, that it would be a dangerous measure, by preserving the unhappy *Norwegians*, to entertain so great a number of enemies within the kingdom. Although the determination, upon which so many miserable wretches must suffer death, is shocking to human nature to think of, yet the *Scotch* were not mistaken in their conjecture; for in less than two months,

months, the Court received information, that a numerous *Danish* fleet had been espied at sea, steering towards *Aberdeen*. As the last army had not yet been much dispersed, they were soon re-collected, and marched with all expedition toward the coast of *Aberdeen*. The *Danes* had but just landed, when *Macbeth* and *Banebo*, again at the head of this army, still flushed with success, fell upon them with such precipitation, that they never got time to form ; the one half of them were cut to pieces, and the other half happy to regain their ships.

' Thus, the *Norwegians* and *Danes* having been both so terribly handled in *Scotland*, they were cooled of any farther designs against that kingdom, which now began to wear the face of peace and prosperity. But as that internal security left too little for ambitious and active spirits to be employed in, their heads were turned upon more selfish objects ; and the uncontrouled actions of the *Ross* faction were now regardless of either right or wrong, any farther than as their proper interests were to be advanced by the one or by the other. They threw off even the disguise of acting for the public weal ; and the whole nation. observing that its wealth and honours were likely to be all amassed into that one family and its dependencies, a general dis-
content

content prevailed, and in a very little time the *Roffian* faction became more odious than at any time had been that of *Caithnefs*.

‘ The Thane of *Rofs* had too much penetration not to perceive it to be his interest to gratify every wifh that could rife in the heart of *Macbeth*; flattering himfelf, that as the affairs of civil adminiftration did not feem at all to tempt the inclinations of *Macbeth*, he had nothing more to do than to keep him from being difgufted, to make fure of his fupport; and with the fupport of *Macbeth*, who had been fo fignally fuccefsful in all his enterprizes, he thought he might domineer over every body elfe. Such a voracious appetite for power, founded too in avarice, could not fail of promoting almoft a general averfion; and the odium againft him grew to fuch a height, that from fecret difapprobation, it arofe to public murmurings.

‘ The fpies of *Caithnefs* continued, from time to time, to communicate to him every tranfaction about the court; and as they rather aggravated than leffened the pictures of difcontentednefs, that fagacious Thane judged it no improper juncture for him and his friends to fhow themfelves once more upon the theatre of action : accordingly *Caithnefs*, with his faft friends, the Thanes of *Sutherland* and *Nairn*, returned to court; and

and the too indolent King being daily teazed
with the cry of grievances which he had
not fpirit to enquire into, and hardly one
courtier of any confequence about him to
whofe confideration he dared to recommend
them, he was at this time very happy in
the return of thefe lords. The welcome
they were received with, very much alarmed the *Roffians*, and political difputers, who
fhould have the ruling of the roaft, for
that, as in other more modern courts, was
the only match to the flame, were renewed
with great violence and inveteracy on both
fides. The many public complaints which
had been for fome time ftifled, now iffued
to the light, and in the beginning gave
great advantage to the *Caithnefs* intereft,
who already began, as the cuftom is, to
turn out and in, to make room for their
own dependants. But as maugre dear
bought experience, they could not diveft
themfelves of that infolence by which they
had formerly forfeited the affections of the
people, the warmnefs with which they were
at firft fupported, did not promife a long
continuance ; *Rofs* and his adherents had
the addrefs to pick our pockets with a courteous bow, and the fmile of complaifance,
whilft thofe of *Caithnefs* purfued the fame
ends, but with the lefs tolerable comportment of pride and infolence. They behaved

as

as if, without giving you caufe to com-
plain, they had a right to opprefs you.

' *Macbeth*, during thefe contentions,
fteered with great dexterity between the
two parties. *Caithnefs*, fenfible to *Macbeth*'s capacity and influence when he had
a mind to employ them, appeared to have
fmothered every former refentment, and
laboured indefatigably to win him to his
intereft : and what was furprizing, confider-
ing the atchievements he had already performed, it neither having entered into the
head of the King nor of *Rofs* to dignify
Macbeth with any honourable title, *Caithnefs* was the firft who had the merit of propofing in council, that *Macbeth*, as an acknowledgment of his great fervices, fhould
be created Thane of *Murray*.

' It was on the fame day that *Caithnefs*
made that popular motion in council, that
Macbeth himfelf communicated to me the
account of a vifion he pretended to have
been vifited with the preceding evening.
' Ruminating (faid he) laft night in my
garden, upon the party diftractions which
divide the Chiefs of this kingdom, without
ever confulting about any meafures that can
tend to make the fubjects either happier,
or the nation itfelf lefs contemptible, I was,
by the gentle murmurs of that purling brook
which glides through it, and the foftening

even

even fongs of drowfy birds, invited to repofe: I had flumbered but a fhort while,
when methought, after a voice like diftant
thunder, not noify but awful, and a profpect of lightening, not glancing nor frightful, but permanent and fhining, there appeared before me three moft angelic female
figures, whofe loofe garments refembled
the waving beams of the fun, and whofe
heads feemed encircled with crowns of ce-
leftial glory. The firft, in paffing, faluted
me with--All hail to *Macbeth*, Thane of
Murray! The fecond, All hail to *Macbeth*,
Thane of *Glamis!* And the third, All hail
to *Macbeth*, King of *Scotland!*' Whether
there was any fuch vifion or no, no body
can determine, but his ambitious wife, to
whom, as to me, he had related it, quickly
raifed upon it the diabolic ftructure, which
from that moment fhe preffed him to execute with fo much vehemence. It has been,
I imagine, upon the foundation of that
vifion, that the ridiculous ftory was invented
of his having been, in the fame language,
faluted by three witches, whom he vifibly
met in a foreft in the middle of a day; and
howfoever much the fiction of the witches
may be better imagined, as better corre-
fponding with the tyrannical conduct which
followed it; yet I will vouch this dream,
as now told by me, to be as it was related
by-

by himself, long before the story of the witches was ever heard of; and I now confider it to have been nothing elfe than the effects of his perpetual thoughts, which incited him to form fuch a dream, to the end that he might obferve the impreffions which thefe epithets carried with them upon the minds of thofe who heard them.

' I am, venerable *Glamis*, (continued *Angus*) the more particular in recapitulating thefe circumftances, that, although you was not altogether a ftranger to them, yet, as your difapprobation of the meafures of all parties, difpofed you, even at that period, to court retirement, and as you could receive information from none, but who, influenced either by the one faction or the other, would reprefent them under fuch falfe colours as were moft for the advantage of the party they leaned to; fo, now that I am no doubt divefted of every temptation to partiality, and had better accefs than almoft any other perfon to know the feveral movements, you will probably be the better enabled to form an ufeful judgment upon the whole.——*Glamis* approved, and *Angus* proceeded.

' It was about the time I laft fpoke of, that your may recollect, there intervened That third party to whom you was inclined

K

to join yourself. This was headed by *Archibald*, the noble Thane of *Argyle*, and who unqueftionably offered his fervices to adminiftration from motives truly patriotic. His family was refpectable, his adherents numerous, and by that influence, fuftained by an excellent underftanding, and principles of unbounded generofity, he flattered himfelf with being able, by advifing an equal diftribution of honours, not regarding names, but the qualities of the perfons, to operate a reconciliation of parties, and that all fhould combine in one, and that one exert itfelf for the public profperity. *Macbeth* had difcernment enough to fee that a perfon of *Argyle*'s power and candid intentions would foon become very popular; and *Argyle* having a more favourable opinion of *Macbeth*'s principles than you, *Glamis*, rather fought than fhunned a connection with him; *Macbeth*, on his part, appeared to efpoufe very warmly every propofition that came from *Argyle*; although he was at the fame time fecretly managing the weak King in fuch a manner as to obftruct, or at leaft to delay the execution of every falutary fcheme, to the end that he might rather aggravate than fuffer to abate that mean opinion which the nobles and gentry in general had long entertained of the unfortunate King. In fhort, by that

confidence

confidence which the *Argathelian* party put
into *Macbeth*, and the countenance of thofe
friends which he artfully contrived to preferve amongft the others, he had now a
much more fplendid court than the neglected *Duncan* himfelf.   At thefe councils
it begun to be whifpered, that the evils into
which the indolent reign of *Duncan* had involved the nation, were become fo obftinate, that a thorough redrefs could hardly
be hoped for under the government of a
Prince fo weak in underftanding, fo fickle
in difpofition, and fo irrefolute in the execution of the beft purpofes; that in fine,
thefe inconveniencies were arrived to fuch
a pitch, that to furmount them required a
King of a daring fpirit, and of a refolution
not to be daunted or diverted.   This was
the very doctrine which *Macbeth* laboured
to inculcate, and upon which he formed
the approaches to his future grandeur.   It
became fo much an adopted maxim of all
or moft of the nobles, that although none
of them chofe to haften it, yet every one
wifhed for the King's death; but there being no great likelihood of that, fome of
them ventured to talk of depofing him,
others to advife him to refign voluntarily.

   ' *Caithnefs*, ever watchful to fuch motions as he imagined he could, by one means
or other, turn to his own purpofes, gave a
hint

hint to the King of the deliberations of the patriotic cabal, and advised him immediately to create his eldest son, *Malcolm*, although but a boy, governor of *Cumberland*, which had, during the several preceding reigns, been reckoned a necessary, and the next step to the crown. This he advised, not only with the view of ingratiating himself with the King, but with the hopes of becoming a sort of regent there during the Prince's minority, and by that measure to gain additional strength to his own power.

' The King actually proposed in council, that his son *Malcolm* should be appointed governor of *Cumberland*; and, without suggesting any body, he added, that how soon the patent was made out, he would name a proper person or persons to be his guardian and assistant in the executive part; as to which, by the advice of *Caithness*, it was his intention to consult the Queen's father, *Sibert*, Duke of *Northumberland*, whom *Caithness* had pre-occupied in his interest.

' The Patriots knew well, that such a proposal had not come spontaneously from the King, but that for certain it must be the scheme of some more active head, in order to disconcert the projects of the new cabal. They were a good deal alarmed, and were of all things anxious to discover
who

who amongſt them could be the perſon
artful and daring enough to throw ſuch a
plauſible obſtruction in the road of their
deſigns. This diſcovery *Macbeth* flattered
himſelf he ſhould be able to make, not by
appearing jealous or inquiſitive, but by
briſkly ſolliciting the King, in the event of
ſuch a patent, that he, as neareſt of kin,
ſhould be appointed governor to the young
Prince. The King was prepared for the
demand, and for once in his life, had the
reſolution to keep his ſecret, and evaded
giving a direct anſwer, by telling *Macbeth*,
that he was not inſenſible to the preference
which was due both to his birth and merit,
but that as he had written for it, he was
determined to come under no engagements
until he had the advice of his father-in-law
the Duke of *Northumberland*. The unuſual
reſolution ſhewn by the King upon this critical occaſion, was more touching to *Macbeth* than all the effect of the intended ap-
pointment, and ſpurred him on to haſten
the determinations of the cabal : pleaſed,
however, that the King, by thus having re-
fuſed him one of the firſt requeſts he had
ever perſonally made in his life, had fur-
niſhed him with a handle for not acting in
concert with him. A general meeting of
the Nobles, or Patriots, as they called
themſelves, were ſoon convened, at which

Caithneſs

Caithnefs attended amongft the reft. They entered warmly upon the uncertain fituation of affairs. *Argyle* obferved, how dangerous it was for any nobleman to rifk his honour and reputation in the fervice of the public, whilft he could not be one day affured but the very beft calculated projects would be defeated the next, by the changeablenefs of the King's temper : that for his part, he would take no fhare in any adminiftration that was not eftablifhed upon a more folid bafis ; and boldly concluded, that although no man prefent had a more loyal and fincere affection for the perfon of the King than himfelf, yet as he had never efteemed him to be well qualified for governing, and that as it was no new thing in that kingdom to fet afide or fufpend for a time the executive power of a King, for the evident advantage and better fecurity of the public, he defired to fubmit it, whether *Duncan*'s Royal authority might not be fufpended, and placed in the hands of fome other, whom the majority of the Nobles fhould judge to be the beft qualified.

' *Macbeth* fpoke next, and, with all the art of an experienced orator, declaimed upon the affecting fenfibility with which he had long beheld the King his kinfman's infirmities : that he had always been obedient to the call of his country when the affiftance

fiftance of his arms were required; but that as affection for the King made him reluctant to cenfure his mode of government, he had very rarely affifted at councils: that it was with forrow he had to obferve, there was yet fome unrevealed meafure of the King's in agitation, which threatened a deeper wound to the independency and conftitution of the nation than any that had hitherto come to light, which was no lefs than a fcheme to over-awe *Scotland* and its Nobles by the power of *Englifh* interpofition; and thereby, continued he, we fhall become no better than a dependency! a province! to that better governed kingdom! If there's any nobleman in this place who is in the fecret of any fuch difgraceful meafure, I fhall expect that he will ftand forth, and, for the honour of his country, make a full difcovery of what he knows; for if ever afterwards it fhould appear, that any one of us have been in fuch a fecret, and fhall not now make the difcovery demanded, I will, for my fhare, at the rifk of my fortune, my fame, and my life, pronounce him to be a traitor, and the betrayer of his country. None of you ftand in a nearer, but one in fo near a connection with the King as myfelf; and yet, without hefitating, be the confequence to *Duncan* as it may, I will openly declare to you the

caufe

cause of my apprehensions. We all know that there has been a motion made to appoint the young *Malcolm* to the government of *Cumberland :* I imagined I had a right to offer my service, as one of his tutors or assistants in that government : I proposed myself to the King, the first boon I had ever personally asked of him ; but how greatly was I astonished, when, in return for all the successful actions of my life, I was coolly told, that that momentous matter was to be directed by a nobleman of the neighbouring kingdom, by *Sibert* Duke of *Northumberland !* The consequences of placing such an important government, so contiguous, so necessary to *England,* and which has been so long the envy of it, into the hands of a powerful *English* nobleman, is too obvious to stand in need of any explanation. I have discharged my conscience of the weight that has lain upon it since the hour I stood alarmed at such a proposal. I leave the remedy with you : and although I will concur in no measure to the personal prejudice of my Sovereign, or his family, I will nevertheless concur in every measure that may better secure the honour, liberty, and independency of this kingdom.——— *Caithness,* conscious that he was pointed at, rose up ; and endeavouring to vindicate the King on the subject of his application to *Northumberland,*

Northumberland, betrayed his being acceſſary to the ſcheme: he excuſed the King, by alledging, that his having written to that Duke on the ſubject, was with no other view, than as he was the Prince's grandfather, and *Cumberland* in the vicinity, not only of *England*, but of the Duke's eſtate, he might, by ſuch an acknowledgment, engage the more his countenance and protection to his grandſon. He owned, that the King had in ſo far communicated to him his intention, but that he could not conceive how any nobleman there ſhould inſinuate that there was any thing traiterous in ſuch a knowledge; and finally, he, as uſual, fell into ſuch a heat, and delivered himſelf with ſo much ſupercilious authority, that his arguments failed of their force, the cabal broke up, the chiefs of it determining, conformable to the wiſh of *Macbeth*, to act no longer in concert with the Thane of *Caithneſs*, or any of his party.

‘ The Lady *Macbeth*, who indefatigably laboured to inſpire her huſband with a paſſion for government, had ſecretly placed herſelf within hearing of theſe debates; and as ſoon as *Macbeth* entered her apartment, ſhe flew to meet him, and caught him in her arms with unuſual ardour. She vowed to him, that until that hour he had never made her half ſo happy; that he had at length

length convinced her that he could speak
from the soul of a man, and that she flattered herself he would prove to her that he
had also the resolution to act so.

' This lady, who had very little of either
the temper of a *Venus* or of a *Juno* in her
composition, was neither troublesome to
her husband in respect of jealousy or of
love. She was of a most uncommon turn
of mind; her ruling passion was for Sway,
and all the rest she made subservient to that
of ambition: her thoughts were so totally
bent upon that one object, that she never
suffered herself to dissolve into the natural
softness of her sex, and was truly incapable
of making herself desireable in amorous enjoyments; insomuch, that as she well knew
that *Macbeth*, with all the martial and aspiring genius which any man could possess,
was nevertheless extremely devoted to the
amorous, she was careful to give him no
sort of interruption in these pursuits; on
the contrary, that his mind might not be
diverted from the Chace which she had in
view, by employing too much of his time
in the other scent, she herself would often
procure for him! Never was there so singu-
lar a character! Thus unweariedly insti-
gated by her, and prompted by his own
inclinations for power, he grew impatient
of uncertainty; he inspirited every one of
the

the cabal with sentiments of the necessity of a revolution; and in a special manner he wrought up *Bancho*, without whose concurrence it would be difficult to enterprize any project more than ordinarily daring, to a settled dislike of the King. He persuaded *Bancho*, that he would act in concert with him, and even give him his influence to supply the place of *Duncan*, as he assured himself he had capacity equal to it. *Bancho*, on the other hand, knew that the preference would be in favour of *Macbeth*; but then, as *Macbeth* had no legitimate issue, nor the probability of getting any with his present wife, he had little doubt but the succession would, at the long run, fall into his family, which *Macbeth* promised to settle by an act of succession, in case the voice of the cabal should declare for him. In fine, an accord was entered into between them to support mutually the schemes of each other.

‘ *Caithness* was no less busy on the other hand in forming counter projects: he persuaded *Duncan*, that he hazarded every thing, if he continued in a place where he was surrounded by a Cabal, who were plotting the destruction of himself and his family: he therefore advised him, in the first place, to send his children, with all possible privacy, into *England*, to the care of their grandfather;

grandfather; and next, to make a sudden
removal of himself to *Inverness*, where he
would be nigher to those only powers who
now remained attached to his interest; that
their forces would be able to protect his
person; and that there was little doubt, in
case the Cabal should dare to proceed, by
violent measures, to set up a king of their
own, but *Northumberland* would have interest enough with the King of *England* to
march some troops to maintain the right of
a family he was so nearly connected to;
which, with those of his own friends from
the northern provinces, might yet be able
to disappoint the undutiful and disloyal projects of the Patriots, as they called themselves. His advice prevailed with the King,
who, without giving any intimation of his
intention to any of the other courtiers, set
out with his family for *Inverness*. As no
body offered to interpose in the least against
his departing, and every thing wore the
face of quietness, *Caithness* apprehending
no danger, left the King on the road, near
the *Blair* of *Athole*, and proceeded to *Inverness*, that he might there the better prepare for his reception.

‘ *Duncan* proposed that night to sleep at
Blair; and although the friends of *Bancho*
have laboured, with every address in their
power, to acquit him entirely of any accession

to

to the affaſſination executed that night upon the King, and to load *Macbeth*, or rather Lady *Macbeth*, with the whole odium of it, yet it was as ſtrenuouſly aſſerted on the other hand, that by whoſoever orders the perpetrators of the maſſacre were employed, yet that ſuch of them as were obſerved to be ſkulking near the houſe that evening, were known to be dependant upon *Bancho* : and if *Macbeth* could be believed, he invariably affirmed to me, that it was a project concerted, without his knowledge, between his wife and *Bancho*. Be that as it may, (for the truth has not, to this hour, come to light) the aſſaſſins performed their bloody buſineſs with determinedneſs and cruelty : they made their way into *Duncan*'s bedchamber in the middle of the night, thro' the blood of the few guards, and every domeſtic that attended upon him ; and ſo inſignificant was he become in the eſteem of his ſubjects, that the murderers retired in the morning, made their eſcape without the leaſt diſcovery, nor was there afterwards any ſort of inquiry ſet on foot to bring them to light.

‘ The news of *Duncan*'s death arriving at *Perth*, *Macbeth* and *Bancho* had a preliminary conference together : they ſent for me, and gave me inſtructions to examine the meſſengers who had brought the ac-

L   counts

counts of the cataſtrophe, and then directed me to ſummon the nobility to aſſemble at *Scoon* the day following.

' *Macbeth* and *Bancho* were amongſt the foremoſt at *Scoon*; they both appeared in mourning, and affected ſo well a concern for the death of the King, that it would have been impoſſible, without being in the ſecret, to have ſuſpected them. Some of the nobles ſaluted *Macbeth* as King upon his firſt appearance, which he as immediately put a ſtop to, declaring, that he pretended to no right but what the voice of the nobles, with the concurrence of the people, ſhould give him : that in point of kinſhip to the deceaſed King, his couſin *Bancho*'s pretenſions were little worſe than his; and he even went ſo far as to ſay, that in many reſpects *Bancho* had ſuperior qualifications for governing; but withal, he artfully concluded, that in ſuch a critical conjuncture, when it was by no means the right of ſucceſſion, but the diſtreſſed ſituation of the country, that was to guide them in their choice, he hoped they would all think as he did, and freely give their voices for that man whom they ſhould account the moſt likely to redreſs their grievances, and to reſtore to the kingdom that credit and reputation which a reign of too much indolence had deprived it of.

He

He faid, he had one nobleman in his eye, whom he regarded as perfectly qualified for that great bufinefs, and named the Thane of *Argyle*. That Thane flood up to fpeak, and probably to declare a determination not to accept, fhould the voices fall upon him, when you, *Glamis*, infifted to be heard. I well remember the ftrength, folidity and juftice, of your reafoning: I fhall, with my lateft breath, blame myfelf for not declaring for your opinion, and regret, that among fo many, there were none who had the honefty and refolution to fupport you. You boldly told the meeting, that you did not imagine they had been conveened there to chufe a King, but a Regent; or Regency; that you could not look upon the Throne as vacant while the deceafed King had children living, who being young, might be educated with proper care, inftructed and trained up to the bufinefs of governing; and that if the nation fhould be fo unhappy as to be difappointed in the abilities of the Princes, that it would be then time enough to elect a King from another family, a meafure at prefent totally unconftitutional, and repugnant to the eftablifhed laws of the kingdom. You was anfwered by *Macbeth*, who argued, that governing according to laws had been for fo many years neglected, it

was

was to remedy thefe neglects that a proper
Ruler was now wanted; that if you would
undertake the regency, and fhould be invefted therein by the ratification of the
ftate, he would very readily concur; but
for his part, he would fooner forfeit his
life than undertake any fhare in the regency
of a kingdom groaning under fuch miferies
and diftractions, as required the beft head,
with the moft refolute heart, to recover it:
that fuch a perfon or perfons muft not be
fhackled by the terror of faction, to be
made refponfible for every action that might
be difagreeable to this or that fyftem of politics: No; it was his opinion, that in fuch
a difficult fituation, no method of government would anfwer the exigencies of the
nation but a *kingly* one, and that King to
be invefted with power uncontroulable;
for otherwife, concluded he, the fame contending parties which fo confoundingly
diftracted the unhappy *Duncan*, will continue, and have it much more in their power
to diftract a powerlefs or fettered Regency.

'*Macbeth* having done, *Rofs*, as the fe-
nior of the Council, rofe up; obferved,
That it was ufelefs to put off time now in
debating about the propriety of what he
imagined had been already determined; it
having been agreed in a former council of
patriots, that the deplorable condition of
the

the nation was fuch, as to demand an immediate and uncommon remedy; and even,
by fufpending the executive authority of
Duncan, and vefting in another the kingly
power, it was judged as then expedient to do
that in his lifetime, the propriety of which
they were now debating about, when his
death made it fo much the more neceffary!
He therefore moved, that they fhould proceed to election; which being agreeable to
the generality of the affembly, they proceeded accordingly, and, by a vaft majority,
Macbeth was chofen King.   He affected to
accept of the royal dignity with great reluctance; he promifed to exert all his underftanding to reform the errors of the paft reign,
and, as much as in him lay, to promote the
general good.   On the fpot he fummoned a
council to attend him next day, and prayed
that every member might be prepared to lay
before him fuch circumftances as moft immediately called for redrefs.

At the meeting next day, you, *Glamis*,
having retired, fent under your feal a fenfible and fpirited proteftation againft the
whole proceedings, which *Macbeth* heard
read without the leaft appearance of refentment: he regretted his not having the concurrence of fo able and honourable a counfellor as *Glamis*, but he hoped that his conduct and actions fhould foon reconcile him,

L 3   and

and every other whofe abfence fpoke them
to be difgufted, to the new meafures of adminiftration. In the mean time, that the
government might diftinguifh its friends
from its enemies, and know who were to
be dreaded, and who to be trufted, he iffued a proclamation, ordaining, that every
nobleman and gentleman fhould, upon a
fixed day at the end of one calender month,
meet in the Council-houfe at *Perth*, on the
pain of being denounced traitors to the ftate.

' Never was a new reign opened with
more applaufe than was that of *Macbeth*;
he fhewed, that he neither would court nor
fear the chiefs of the different parties, but
diftinguifhed them by honours and favour
according to their refpective merits: he
inftantly eftablifhed regular courts of juftice, and the people began to be charmed,
by now feeing a due adminiftration of right,
of which they had been fo long deprived.
He was the premier judge of every court
himfelf, and often attended when his prefence was leaft expected; fo that property
was fecured with impartiality, and oppreffion was punifhed with unawed feverity.
The remiffnefs of former government had
encouraged the moft wicked of the people
to prey upon their peaceable neighbours,
and avowed gangs of thieves kept open and
daring affemblies, to contrive how they
might

might with impunity moſt ſuccefsfully forn
upon, and pillage from thoſe parts of the
country where they feared no reſiſtance.
In a word, it not being worth the while of
the induſtrious to improve their poſſeſſions,
as they could not be ſure of enjoying the
effects of their labour; huſbandry was totally neglected, and deſolation threatened
to cover the face of the earth: robbers and
pillagers were become ſo numerous, that all
communication from one part of the kingdom to another was interrupted, none daring to journey without the eſcort of ſuch a
force as few were able to maintain; nay,
many of the public officers had been corrupted by the thieves; and thoſe whoſe
duty it had been to give a check to the depredations, connived at them. *Macbeth*
made a general removal amongſt all the
out-parties, and replaced them by ſuch
troops, with officers over them, as he was
certain would execute his orders. Theſe
ſalutary meaſures drove the thieves into
more remote parts, and they formed into
greater bodies; he employed truſty emiſſaries to mingle with them, and by that
means they were often led into ſnares out
of which there was no eſcaping. At length
he contrived, by one *grand coup*, and the
force of money, of which he was very li-
beral, to ſubdue them entirely; he engaged
his

his emissaries amongst them to harrangue
them into an opinion that they could not
now subsist long upon paultry pilfering;
that they would do well to catch the first
favourable opportunity of striking one important blow, which should enable them to
chuse for themselves some one district of
the country the most impregnable, and
there, in an united body, to live and defend
themselves maugre all resistance. To this
end he had it given out, that the whole
treasures of *Ross*, *Inverness*, the Islands,
and *Argyleshire*, were to be collected, and,
under different inconsiderable escorts, to be
brought down, for the greater security, to
Edinburgh : that all the parties were to rendezvous at *Blair*, and there to deliver over
their charge to one treasurer, whom the
King was to send out to meet them for that
purpose; that then the several escorts were
to be relieved, and sent back to their respective homes : that nothing would be
easier than for the chiefs of the ravagers,
unknown to the multitude, to manage their
matters so, as to assemble by partial parties
through the mountains in the neighbourhood of *Blair*, and, upon an agreed signal,
to form into one body, to fall upon the
King's escort, and make themselves masters
of the whole treasure, with which they
might with safety retire to any place to be
considered

confidered upon for their future eftablifhment. This plaufible device had its effect, and the chiefs of the banditti formed a plan by which to execute it. *Macbeth* being duly informed of all this, took his meafures, by difpatching empty carriages into different parts, which were fuppofed, as intended to return loaded, to give the impofition the greater air of probability; and in the mean time he had prepared a fufficient number of his chofen troops, to be fituated in convenient ambufhes, from whence they were to iffue at an appointed moment, and furround the plunderers. This ftratagem had every effect his heart could defire; it was executed to a point; the robbers were totally defeated; and as many of them as were not flain in the enterprize, were brought in prifoners to *Scoon,* and there made proper examples of.

' The unexperienced tranquillity in which the middling and common people now lived throughout the country, diftinguifhed the beginning of this reign with numberlefs encomiums, and added fuch ftrength to the hands of *Macbeth,* that he had nothing to fear.

' In confequence of his proclamation, almoft every man of confequence, *Glamis* excepted, appeared at court. The Thanes of *Caithnefs, Sutherland,* and *Nairn,* alfo returned,

returned, and tendered their allegiance; they were received, and even embraced. But

' The reftlefs *Roffians*, now finding that their influence had dwindled almoft to nothing, began to foment frefh difturbances. The Thane, arrogating the chief merit of feating *Macbeth* upon the throne, having propofed his eldeft fon, who by this time affumed the air of a man of the firft confequence, to be general in chief of the troops, the King refufed his requeft, upon the footing of the young *Rofs* not having fufficiency of experience for fuch a command. The Thane thought himfelf flighted, and from that moment nourifhed the feeds of refentment. *Caithnefs* perceived the coolnefs with inexpreffible fatisfaction, and to make the moft timely advantage of it, preffed his fervice in every fhape upon *Macbeth*. He knew them and their practices too well to fuffer the Crown to fall under the tutelage of either of them : he declared he would have no favourites ; that the beft fervice he could do his country, was to difcountenance all parties ; that follicitations for power or places fhould have no effect upon him ; that he would look through his own eyes, and promote fuch only, who in his impartial judgment fhould be beft qualified to fill the places they were to occupy for the public good. He defired they might

not

not interpret his declared purposes as they had been accustomed to interpret the too good-natured *Duncan*'s, mere words, without a meaning, or he should convince them of the contrary, by punctually executing whatsoever had been once in his mind determined. Neither of the old factions having been used to, nor relishing such cavalier treatment, were equally offended, and for once joined their heads together in the formation of projects to perplex *Macbeth*'s administration. They retired in disgust into their respective countries, resolving to invite the return of young *Malcolm*, and in case he should refuse, to make a trial upon *Bancho*, or any other who should be more ductile than they had found *Macbeth*. Manifesto's were now published in support of the lawful heir, and in opposition to such lawless usurpation, as threatened to terminate in the ruin of nobility. Such well-sounding pretences induced some, but a propensity to fish in troubled waters incited many more, who had been long accustomed to uncontrouled oppression and rapine, to join in the cry of these discontented Thanes. Amongst the malecontents, there were men of extensive property, and a most numerous dependence, which enabled them to prepare for the field a formidable

dable power, at the head of which they soon displayed a royal standard.

' *Macbeth* was not asleep during these operations, but mustered an army, which he flattered himself should be sufficient to put a check to their designs: to this army he appointed the noble Thane of *Argyle* to the next command with himself; and to be before-hand with any countenance they might hope for from *England*, he ordered *Argyle* to march directly with the first division, consisting of about 4000 men, and he followed the next day at the head of 6000, leaving *Bancho* to the direction of affairs at home, and to have an eye to the southward, in case of any motions from the *English* side. *Argyle* marched straight towards the enemy's rendezvous, who were astonished to find by his advancing, that *Macbeth* had been so unexpectedly expeditious in collecting a body to oppose them; but having reconnoitred, and discovering the advanced division not to exceed 4000, they determined, although their force had not all come in, to advance, and give them battle immediately. *Argyle* having intelligence of their intention, made a halt on advantageous ground, to wait the King's arrival; but early next morning, and before the King could come up, he was saluted with a violent attack; he disputed his
ground

ground againſt their ſuperior numbers with
amazing prudence and intrepidity, for almoſt two hours, when *Macbeth*'s arrival
with the ſecond diviſion quickly decided
the combat. The enemy, now preſſed,
not only with ſuperior courage, but with
ſuperior numbers, were put into the ut-
moſt confuſion; they were totally routed;
a terrible carnage attended it; every one of
the leaders, excepting the old Thane of
Roſs, who was killed, were made priſoners;
but by my interpoſition, ſeconded by *Ar-*
gyle, the common people did not meet with
the cruel fate which deſtroyed the rebels in
Skie; the moment victory was aſcertained,
quarter in general was proclaimed for ſuch
ſubjects as ſhould throw down their arms.

' The whole northern provinces being
now ſubdued, *Macbeth* made proper ſettle-
ments, under the government, of ſuch officers as he could confide in, and returned to
Perth in high triumph. The next queſtion
of conſequence was, What ſteps ſhould be
taken with regard to the ring-leaders of the
laſt inſurrection? Few of the council appeared diſpoſed to puniſh capitally ſo many
men of the firſt quality; but Lady *Mac-*
beth, now the *Queen*, always bent on extirpation of enemies; and although her own
brother, the young Thane of *Roſs*, was one
of the principal delinquents, founded no-

M   thing

thing but execution in the King's ear : she had a mighty influence over him, notwith-standing which, the concurring endeavours of *Bancho*, *Argyle* and myself, would have prevailed, had not, unluckily for these noblemen, news arrived very *mal-a-propos* that *Macgild*, the most powerful baron of *Galloway*, had put himself at the head of a formidable rising in these parts ; this news conspiring with the impressions of the Queen, determined the fate of the Chiefs ; and accordingly the Thanes of *Ross, Caithness, Sutherland* and *Nairn*, were all ordered for execution, and lost their heads early the day following.

' The execution of these noblemen was no sooner over, than the King once more put himself at the head of a gallant army ; and leaving *Bancho* and *Argyle* to conduct matters at home, he carried me with him, the second in command upon that expedition. He made most fatiguing and incredible marches with part of the army, in hopes to arrive timely enough to prevent any communication between the insurgents on this and the other side of the river *Annan* ; but not being able to accomplish that, and his men being insupportably fatigued, he had been worsted in two several skirmishes ; after which, in the night, *Macgild*, being much better acquainted with

that

that country than he, had laid a fcheme to furround him, and make him and his people prifoners before morning. *Macgild* had executed his fcheme with abundance of dexterity; and whilft *Macbeth* was manfully ftruggling in the toils he was caught in, I, who fortunately had advanced half a day fafter than he expected, came up to his relief, and cutting my way thro' the rear of the enemy, threw my troops into the heat of the action. Upon my arrival *Macbeth* was almoft quite fpent, but re-infpired with frefh vigour, and re animating his half defponding troops, we jointly affailed the enemy with fuch irrefiftible force, that in lefs than half an hour a complete victory declared for us. *Macgild* was wounded, and taken prifoner; I petitioned for his life, but in vain; *Macbeth* urging, that while fuch turbulent fpirited men were alive, he fhould have no time to effect that reformation in the civil and political government of the nation which he was fo anxious to accomplifh; but, as a proof that he was not infenfible to the timely fuccour I had brought him that day, he drew his fword, held it by the point, and delivering it to me, created me Thane of *Angus*, a title never before beftowed out of the royal family. That ceremony being quickly over, and he accepting of my fword in place of his own,

he

he enjoined, that in neither words, looks or actions, I should shew the smallest disapprobation of his next orders: he elevated, with such implements as he could find, a scaffold, which he ordered should be encircled by the prisoners, and commanded them to shout with acclamations of joy, when, at the sound of a trumpet, the executioner should sever the head from the body of the arch-rebel their leader; promising them, that, as he should discover their satisfaction to be real or counterfeited, he would deal with them accordingly: he regarded them, as far as his eye could comprehend them, with great exactness himself, and he had agents mingled with them to report as to those he could not see. How soon the execution of *Macgild* was over, he ordered all the prisoners to be drawn up in right lines before him, and picking out those who had been least affected, and loudest in their huzzas, he also ordered them for immediate execution, declaring aloud, that those villains who could be so indifferent about the fate of a master whom they knew, and had sworn to serve, could never be faithful to another whom they did not know; and as he was resolved to take the rest under his protection, and employ them in his service, he should hope, that as they had felt for the suffering of a master who

who had misled them into rebellion and
disgrace, they would adhere still more faith-
fully to one who would never lead them but
in search of glory and honour. This con-
ceit, uncommon as it was, had an amazing
effect upon the minds of the fellows who
were saved, and who attached themselves
ever after so closely to him, that they were
the very last soldiers he had to depend upon.

' By such uninterrupted successes and
resolute discipline, he effectually humbled
all the spirit of turbulency for a time, and
was now in a condition to establish a peace
upon a pretty solid footing ; for by these
arts, and an awful, although discreet, deportment, he found himself, after his return, not only rivetted in the esteem of the
nobility, but in the affections of the people,
which for a considerable time he improved,
by framing and governing by a number of
more useful and wholesome laws than had
been known in the days of almost any of
his predecessors.

' If accidents had occurred to occupy
that activity of soul which prompted him
to noble and warlike atchievements, he
might have longer continued in the character of a great man ; but an uninterrupted
tranquillity leaving him now too much at
his ease, and as, if his mind was not employed in one pursuit, it must in another,

so

fo now libidinous, began to fucceed to martial exploits; and as his Queen was a woman who took no fort of delight in conjugal, or in any kind of amorous embraces,
but had rather an averfion to mankind in
that particular; and as the ambition of her
foul was to govern, fhe often ftarted game
for her hufband, that while fhe might engage his attention to thefe objects, fhe
might enjoy to herfelf the greater pleafure
of regulating the affairs of court.

‘ As fhe was ambitious, fo fhe was extremely jealous of her power; fhe could
not bear the thoughts of any perfon living
at eafe, whom fhe fufpected to have the
moft remote chance of fharing power
with her: the recollection that *Bancho* had
fo much as been named, along with her
hufband, as a competitor for the diadem, preyed conftantly upon her fpirits:
fhe confidered every piece of refpect that
was paid to his modefty and merit, as de-
tracting from *Macbeth*; and fome of her
creatures having, undefignedly, informed
her, that it had been prognofticated to
Bancho by certain gipfies, “ that he or his
pofterity fhould one day be Kings of *Scotland*, and that the fucceffion fhould remain
in his family as long as the nation ftood;”
her imagination was impreffed with an un-
conquerable averfion to him: fhe placed
fpies

ſpies upon all his actions, in hopes of becoming miſtreſs of ſome ſcandal that might
promote enmity between him and the King ;
but the prudent uniformity by which
Bancho ſquared his conduct, baffled every
hope that way : ſhe would ſometimes pro-
poſe to herſelf to alarm the pride of the
King, by giving him a hint of the prophecy,
but then ſhe thought too well of *Macbeth*'s
underſtanding, to ſuppoſe that ſuch a frivo-
lous ſtory could influence him to break
with a man, of whoſe fidelity and friendſhip
he had got ſuch inconteſtable proofs. Hell
at length aſſiſted her, and ſuggeſted the
means of opening a breach between the two
friends. About this time *Bancho* had unfortunately introduced to court *Inetta*, a half-
ſiſter of his, a young lady not leſs admirable for unequalled beauty, than ſhe was
eſteemed for a ſhining underſtanding ; a-
dorned with ſo much modeſty of behaviour,
that by every body ſhe was beloved, but
rather ſentimentally than paſſionately : ſhe
lived at *Bancho*'s houſe, and from his rela-
tionſhip and connection with *Macbeth*, his
ſiſter *Inetta* ſoon became familiar in the
Queen's parties. The Queen, with perhaps the moſt vicious heart that was ever
lodged in the breaſt of a woman, had an
amazing faculty of ſmothering the cor-
ruptibleneſs of it ; and by an admirable
dexterity

dexterity in diffimulation, fhe could pafs
for the virtuous or vicious, for the conde-
fcending or infolent, for the diffipated or
rigid ; and, in fhort, could affume the con-
traft of all that was good, or all that was
bad, juft as the one or the other beft fuited
her company ; in fo much, when at any
time circumftances prejudicial to her fame
had by accident tranfpired, thofe of the
moft unfufpected reputations appeared
ready to defend her.

'The innocent *Inetta*, unfufpicious of ill,
had exerted every amiable quality fhe was
miftrefs of, to render herfelf agreeable to
the Queen ; who on her part, was as anxi-
oufly meditating how fhe might turn her
acquaintance with this beautiful young creature to the ruin of herfelf, and the deftruction of her brother and his family. To this
wicked purpofe fhe embraced the firft favourable opportunity of reprefenting fuch
a picture of her to *Macbeth*, as could not
fail to awaken his paffions with the warmeft
prepoffeffions in her favour, and with an
immediate defire to fee her : the Queen
promifed to gratify his longing very foon ;
and accordingly, upon a day when fhe knew
that Lady *Bancho* was to be otherwife engaged, fhe requefted, that as fhe was
determined to fee no other company,
Lady *Bancho* would difpenfe with the attendance

tendance of *Inetta*, and allow her to pass
the day at her apartments: Lady *Bancho's*
consent was as sure to be obtained as asked;
and thus the plan was prepared for dishonouring the fair *Inetta*, under the colour
of doing her the greatest honour that the
preference of a Queen could confer. *Macbeth*, on pretence of retiring from the fatigue of business, to divert an hour with the
Queen, whom he imagined, as he said, was
alone, entered without any ceremony into
the chamber where she and *Inetta* were
amusing themselves: he saw her, and at
first sight stopping short, he addressed his
wife---I imagined, my dear, said he, you was
alone; my eyes convince me that you are
not alone; but whether it is a human creature or an angel you are happy with, my
senses cannot yet distinguish! pray unde-
ceive me: the Queen told him, smiling,
that his eyes were not often mistaken;
then taking *Inetta* by the hand, who had
respectfully raised herself to salute the King,
bid him not be afraid, for if her companion
was an angel, she was a corporeal one, and
in that same angel he might embrace a
cousin, in the person of *Inetta*, sister to his
friend *Bancho*! *Macbeth*, more touched
with that awful and unaffected modesty
which were the distinguishing ornaments of
Inetta's charms, than he had ever been with
any

any beauty before, advanced and faluted
her, but rather with a courtly decency than
that kingly ftatelinefs which he wore upon
other occafions: he immediately fell into
converfation with her; and if he was at firft
fight ftruck with her figure, ne was now no
lefs tranfported with that fenfibility and dignity with which fhe modeftly delivered herfelf upon every fubject. The Queen made
many errands to give them an opportunity
of being *tête a tête*, and on fuch occafions
Macbeth would make fly advances, to guefs
at the pulfations of her heart; all of which
ferved no other purpofe, but the more to
convince him that fhe was of a very different complexion from any of thofe to whom
he had formerly tendered his addreffes.
Such diftant, tho' courteous deportment,
the more enhanced the value of her charms,
and infpired him with a greater ardour to
enjoy them; though the refpect which her
manner commanded, made him keep a very
tight rein over his glowing paffion. The
Queen was happy to obferve how well her
fcheme went forward, but wifhed to fee the
King's defires inflamed to a greater violence.

' *Inetta* having taken leave, the Queen
rallied her hufband with having been rather
a whining than a manly lover; he accounted for that, by telling her, that if he was
not much miftaken, *Inetta* poffeffed per-
fections

fections that were not to be fubdued by
ftorm ; that all the game which had hitherto been ftarted for him, were, in compari-
fon of *Inetta*, fit only for the chafe of potch-
ers ; but the lovely and accomplifhed *Inetta*
was truly worthy the purfuit of monarchs !
The Queen, not fo well contented with that
ferious manner in which he treated this
amour, revolving in her mind how fhe
might ftir up his paffion to more intempe-
rate emotions ; told him, that as he had yet
but half feen the beauties of *Inetta*, fhe
would contrive to gratify every fenfe with
a more complete perfpective of them : I
intend to-morrow, faid the Queen, to engage her to bathe with me, and from the
inlet of light over the door of the bath,
which I will leave unlatched, you may get
an opportunity of feafting your eyes with
the whole object, as mafterly nature finifhed
it : *Macbeth* was in extacy with the thought,
and in the utmoft impatience waited for
the hour that was to prefent fuch delight to
his fight : the moment arrived, and by this
malign plot of *Margaretta*'s, the whole
charms of the innocent and unfufpecting
Inetta were difcovered in their native beau-
tifulnefs ! At that inftant he would have
bartered his life and crown, to have had the
power of retaining his fenfes, and to be at
the fame time transformed into a bladder of
air

air, or a curl of water! If he was captivated before, he now raved! he had no ideas that were not filled with *Inetta!* and he was determined not to live many hours without the possession of her! Business, company, every thing became disgustful to him: to me alone he communicated the earnings of his soul; and I shall never forget his pathetic representation of the bathing scene, from which an able painter might have described a *Venus*, exquisitely finer than any thing yet produced by poetic imagination! Believe me, *Glamis*, I employed all the force of my tongue and understanding to divert him from the pursuit of an intrigue, which already looked big with interruptions of inquietude and horror; derogatory to his interest, honour and reputation; and above all, injurious and ruinous to the peace, fame and fortune, of a young lady whom he owned was worthy of the first diadem on earth; and whom, by all the rules of honour and hospitality, it was his duty to protect: in fine, I urged the breach of every thing sacred in friendship, and expressed my amazement, that those close ties that had so long and warmly connected him to the noble *Bancho*, did not upbraid him for entertaining the most remote thought of dishonouring his family! But I might as well have preached to the winds; his

passions

paffions were up; and when they were fo, he was ever deaf to argument: upon this occafion he checked the liberty I had taken with more heat than I had hitherto experienced; I then foftened my mode of reafoning, and hoping at leaft to defer his impetuofity, I recommended to him an affiduous application of fair means; obferving, that there were few women, how much foever obftinate in the beginning, that had refolution with firmnefs to oppofe the charms of royalty in an adorer, efpecially when the moft favourable opportunities could not be wanting to enforce importunity. I told him, that violence would procure but half enjoyment, and bid him coolly afk himfelf, how different he fhould efteem the delights which *Inetta* was capable of beftowing voluntarily, and thofe which in tears and diftraction he might be able to ravifh from her: I gained fome attention to this fort of reafoning, which I improved to the beft advantage in my power. He fought every occafion of being in her company; and the profligate Queen, that fhe might forward the rapacious defign, always contrived they fhould be left alone. According to my advice, he had command enough of himfelf to begin by gradual advances; and *Inetta* apprehending no ill, entertained him with a difcreet

N   freedom;

freedom; until one day he turned the converfation upon the *honour of the sex*, which
he treated very lightly, and as no more
than an ufeful phrafe to defend them againft
attacks of pleafure, when they difliked the
object. *Inetta* began to be alarmed, and
pled the caufe of her fex with fuch uncommon fpirit, as rather excited than extinguifhed his flame : with eyes fparkling
love, and emotions boiling with defire, he threw himfelf at her feet, told her
how miferable he was to be deprived of the
power of making his mind known to her,
by means which honour might juftify;
that maugre all reftraint, he could not
longer fmother the labouring fecret; and
that unlefs fhe gave him leave to hope,
he muft make a wretched example of himfelf! He grafped her fo faft, there was no
efcaping; he preffed ardent kiffes upon her
trembling hand; thence he rofe to her
fhivering lips, and, amidft a variety of
ftrugglings, without giving her time to
utter a word, he ravifhed numberlefs kiffes!
At length fhe difentangled herfelf, and was
flying from his arms, when the Queen
thought fit to enter; fhe faw the confufion,
and afking what was the matter, the King,
affuming a jocular fort of air, replied, Nothing at all, my dear, but that I have been
robbing the delicious lips of *Inetta* of fome
sweet

sweet kisses, which she had very ill will to part with; she thinks me, I suppose, too old for such favours! *Inetta* imagining, with justice, that the Queen would load her husband with reproaches for the violent freedom he had taken, waited, with anxious impatience, for her reply; but how greatly was she astonished to hear the Queen observe, that *Inetta* was but young at court, else she would put a higher value upon the kisses of a King; especially, added she, when so innocent, my Lord, as I suppose your's to have been; a little Platonic love from a King, is what the most scrupulous lady may admit of!——And all other love, replied *Macbeth*, being your due, my Queen, I flattered myself, that neither you nor *Inetta* would disapprove of a little harmless amusement.

' I like not, answered *Inetta*, to play with even the preliminaries of love, which, although perhaps not criminal in themselves, will be interpreted otherwise by the world; the King's Platonic addresses I shall not presume to judge of; but as the warmth with which he enforced them, was of that nature, that I should have resented with indignation, had they been offered by the greatest subject of the kingdom; so even from the King they have left such an impression upon me, that however duti-

N 2   **fully**

fully I respect him, yet I shall confess I have a greater regard for my own reputation and peace of mind; and therefore, unless I can be assured that I shall not be persecuted with any more of them, I must beg leave to retire from the court: the King, and you, Madam, will the more readily approve my resolution, that the honour I have of being related to him ought to inspire me with a caution to risk nothing that may be inconsistent with that high blood which flows through my veins; and if I ever should hearken to love, even the love of a King! it shall be one who has the power of offering with it a crown!

' The Queen affected to applaud her resolution, although she could very ill stomach the dignity with which she concluded what she had said; nay, she began to be susceptible to a fear, that the very fire which she had been so industrious to kindle, might arrive to such a pitch, as might terminate in her own ruin: she knew that *Macbeth* was not to be baffled, after he had resolved; she saw how desperately he was in love, and apprehended that he would try to obtain the enjoyment, let the purchase be ever so dear to him; she therefore determined, that as there was no security for herself, but by obtaining the gratification of the King's passion upon any terms,

if

if the fair *Inetta* was not to be fubdued, by the ordinary fnares formed to
conquer virtue, to betray her into compliance. She foothed the King as well,
in the mean time, as fhe could ; fhe
intreated him to be patient for a few days,
and undertook at the peril of her life, by
one mean or other to acomplifh his happinefs.

' The King however not feeing the idol of
his foul as ufual, grew penfive and melancholy ; it was impoffible to entertain him.
Bancho furprifed him one day whilft he was
walking and mufing in his palace garden :
and as a friend, intreated to know the caufe
of his difcontent? *Macbeth* tried in his prefence to put on an appearance of greater
compofure, but the emotions of his heart
would not difguife for him : *Bancho* preffed
him the more earneftly, to let him at leaft
fhare in what diftreffed him, declaring if
he fhould not have the power to alleviate it,
he fhould certainly lighten the burthen by
bearing a part of it.——He told *Bancho* that
he of all others, was the leaft likely to
affift him, and therefore defired he might
defift from inquiring into the knowledge
of what if once known, would give him
pain, and rather, if poffible add to, than
leffen his own. *Bancho* little dreaming
what could be the caufe, ftill perfifted;

yea,

yea, conjured him by all the ties of facred friendfhip, to difclofe his mind, with an afleveration, that if his life and fortune could reftore to him that tranquility, which fome malignant fpirit had rob'd him of, he might command them: Well then, friend *Bancho*, faid *Macbeth* you fhall know, and many other men in your place would purchafe my relief, although you who alone can do it, will I am almoft certain, refufe it ; Know too inquifitive friend, that I love! that, to diftraction I love ! thy adorable fifter, the fair *Inetta !* You have faid you would purchafe my quiet at the expence of your life and fortune ; you may if you dare, befriend me without the forfeit of either. *Bancho*, like one thunder ftruck, hefitated to reply. At length recovering himfelf; I little thought faid he, that the Wound could point there ! I did fay, I could facrifice my life to your repofe, but you cannot think I would my honour ! No ! *Macbeth* would not permit, that *Bancho* fhould confpire in proftituting to luft a fifter ! a virgin of your own blood ! You have not fo poor an opinion of my virtue !—*Bancho ! Bancho !* faid the King, I know well thy virtue in love affairs ; and that on other occafions it has been thy maxim, That the love of a fine woman diffolves all connections and

con-

considerations whatever. But no more of that : a flight ftruck out, only, to try the firmnefs of your virtue, which I am afraid will rife with equal repugnance, when I open to you, the true fcource of my melancholy meditations. I have told you that it is you alone who can operate m relief; but that you of all other men will probably the moft oppofe it. My fouls anxiety then my dear *Bancho* continued he, nicely endeavouring to turn off the attention from his filter, fprings from the misfortune of my having no children; the people I imagine are always difcontented, under a barren reign; and although next to my wife, I have the greateft affection for your family, yet I confefs I fhall never be eafy, unlefs I can fee a chance of being fucceeded by either one of my own, or one of my wifes body; I have had, and may have children of my own body, but thefe the law of the land exclude. My wife is, to appearance, as likely to have children as any other woman, and therefore I have long thought that a change of the culture, might effect, what my conftant toil has never been able to produce. I have faid, that you are the fingle man on earth who can affift me; but the only man whom I am afraid will not confent to the means; I fay, the only one who can

affift

affift me, becaufe there is not another in life, to whom I would truft a fecret of fo much importance; and yet the only one whofe confent I cannot expect, becaufe of difappointing your own pofterity. Thus did this artful man, as had been before hand concerted between him, and the as artful Queen, give a very fpecious turn off, to his bafe defigns upon the virtuous *Inetta*; when he found that her Brother was not to be feduced, to be an accomplifh, in fuch a difhonourable fcene of debauchery.

'*Bancho* was no lefs amazed at the laft, than with the former propofal: He told the King, his language was beyond all comprehenfion; that he certainly fpoke in paradoxes; but if they were to have no other end, than to divert his melancholy, he was happy in being the object of them: *Macbeth* ftudied as much as in him lay, to perfuade *Bancho* that it was the affair of his own family, and nothing regarding *Inetta*, which was the caufe of his difcompofure: *Bancho* however reafoned with him, as to the impropriety of that project alfo, fuppofing it could have entered into his head; and argued, that if he was to prevail with any perfon whatfoever to undertake fo unheard of, and hazardous an attempt, the confequence would be rather to difquiet him

him the more, than in the leaſt to tranqui-
life him : ſo for this time they parted
neither of them very well contented : *Macbeth* was unhappy in his unſucceſsful endeavours with *Bancho* ; and *Ban ho* could
not help, being greatly alarmed with ap-
prenſions on account of his ſiſter. He immediately went to find her, and when he
learnt from herſelf, what had paſſed between her and the King, he was confirmed
in his fears ; for although the indifferent
part the Queen had acted in the ſcene,
had a good deal compoſed the fears of
the unſuſpicious *Inetta*, yet *Bancho* who
had more experience in the machinations
of mankind, was very much diſturbed in
his mind about it ; it was therefore reſolved
between them, that *Inetta* ſhould embrace
the very firſt opportunity of retiring into
the country, without ſaying one word
about it, until ſhe ſhould be ready to take
her leave. *Macbeth* on his part having
diſcloſed every article of the converſation
to his wife, who was keen in the project of
enticing *Bancho* to her bed ; rather to ſa-
tisfy a helliſh, than a fond guſt of paſſion recommended it to him, to renew his applications with earneſtneſs, to gain that end ; and
I promiſe you, ſays ſhe, that the ſame night
that you can engage *Banco* to attempt my
bed, you ſhall be received into that of *Inetta*.
Macbeth

Macbeth now shutting not only his eyes but his understanding to every principle of honour, friendship or humanity ; and aggravating in idea the resentment he had awakened in *Bancho*. on account of an avowed design upon his sister ; prompted by the most ungovernable lust for her ! and considering him as an almost invincible of obstruction to the completion of his happiness : he resolves to pursue his wife's advice, let the consequences be what they may. He, therefore, in a fit of real languor and perturbation of mind, sends for *Bancho* to attend him in his closet, and there renewed the discourse upon the misery he suffered, and which preyed every day, he said so much deeper and deeper upon his spirits ; that it was become quite insupportable to him : he continued, by telling him that he had even mentioned his proposal regarding *Bancho* to the Queen, who although at first much discomposed by it, was at length so moved by the distress she saw him in, that he did not doubt of reconciling her soon to the experiment proposed, extraordinary as it was ! so that now my friend, concluded he, the peace, or wretchedness of your King and friend, is entirely depending upon you. The gravity with which he delivered himself upon this occasion, made some impression upon *Bancho* ; who

fearing

fearing that every objection he might oppose to it, would be interpreted as springing from self interestedness, appeared rather consenting than averse to the design: but withal, hoping still to procure a delay, he urged, that if the Queen should be prevailed with, to commit such an uncommon violence, against decency and inclination; yet, that he the King, should undoubtedly have left the choice of her object entirely to herself: *Macbeth* replied, that he had truly done so; and that as it was an intrigue prompted by no sort of passion, but merely an affair of expediency, her opinion coincided in every respect with his; that in an endeavour of so vast importance, where the honour and credit of the kingdom, with her personal fame and reputation were the valuable stakes, if there was any man on earth deserving of such a confidence, it must be *Bancho*. *Bancho* could not easily conquer a variety of doubts which sprung in his mind; but he had heard too much; he knew not how to recede. *Macbeth* perceived he was hesitating, and fearing the plot should misgive, began to upbraid him, with want of friendship, and insensibility to the honour proposed to him. *Bancho* assured the King, that in point of friendship no man ever felt its impressions stronger than he;

and

and the honour of prefering him to the Queen's bed was undoubtedly unexampled, but withal he said, it was an honour of such an extraordinary nature, and charged with such hazards in the execution, that for his foul he could not tell how he fhould mufter up a fufficiency of affurance, to make a tender of his perfon, to a Queen whom he had never approached but with veneration. *Macbeth* bid him be perfectly eafy on that fcore ; that every thing fhould be fo conducted, as that he fhould enjoy the pleafure, or perform the duty, which ever he chofe to think it, without the expence of one blufh. In fine ; *Bancho* at laft, tho' very reluctantly, promifed to be at the King's difpofal, and to proceed in the affair as he fhould be by him directed.

    ' *Macbeth* now haftens to greet his Lady with the fuccefs, and to remind her of the promife to accomplifh his fruition in the confequence : She had already prepared for the event, in her imagination, ever fertile in mifchiefs ! An aniverfary feftival was at hand, fhe plans the execution of her dire intent for that night. In the interval, the King having affumed a more regular and eafy appearance, than had been obferved for fome days paft ; and having commanded even his looks, from betraying any fymptons alarming to *Inetta* :
Bancho

Bancho actually began to banish the alarms he had entertained upon her account, and to believe that the King's uneasiness had really proceeded from the ridiculous cause he had himself assigned for it, and was therefore less solicitous about her departure from court, than otherwise he would have been.

' Upon the morning of the fatal day, that Lady *Macbeth* had destined for the most unnatural tragedy that ever was acted, *Macbeth* called upon *Bancho* in the morning, and telling him, that that was to be the night, which he hoped would beget him an heir for his Kingdom, he invited him, with his family, to commemorate the feast, which was his own birth-day, at the palace ; and, says he, that you may be under no sort of apprehensions of committing any disagreeable surprise upon the Queen, and to prevent the blushes of either of you, I will myself conduct you into, and help to undress you in the bed-chamber! And to give the most natural look to the whole, continued he, that neither the domesticks of your house, nor of the palace, may make any suspicious observations, I will at supper publicly insist, that you, your son and sister, may all sleep in the Palace for the night. *Bancho* was now too deeply en-

O   gaged

gaged, to diſſent from any thing he propoſed, and therefore went about making
the neceſſary preparations to partake of a
feſtivity, which was to be crowned with
the deſtruction of himſelf and family.

'Never was there a more ſplendid court,
than came to ſolemnize that anniverſary ;
the day was ſpent in the height of luxury
and joy, nor was there the leaſt room left,
for the moſt prying eye to ſuſpect that it
could end otherwiſe than as it had begun ;
only, as if providence had meant to diſ-
appoint the blood thirſty Queen in her
hopes of annihilating a whole race, which
was her mercileſs deſign ; young *Fleans*,
Bancho's ſon, was taken ſo ſuddenly ill,
that it was neceſſary to carry him home,
and which accident had well nigh defeated
the whole project ; for the tender hearted
Inetta, who doated on her nephew with a
parental fondneſs, would not participate
in any of their diverſions, but inſiſted on
attending him home, until it ſhould be
ſeen what turn his illneſs might take.
This interruption threw ſuch a cloud of
heavineſs over their enjoyments, and more
over ſome of their expectations, that the
face of things was changed from gaiety
to ſadneſs. *Macbeth* counterfeited a prodigious concern for *Fleans*, and would not
reſt ſatisfied, unleſs he went in perſon to

fee how it was with him; and that he might leave no room with *Bancho* to imagine that he had any fort of inclination to catch *Inetta* alone, he moft artfully defired *Bancho* to go with him; which he as readily complied with. They found *Fleans* fo well recovered, that he might have rejoined the company, but his phyfician difuaded it: the reft however all returned immediately to the palace, and there renewed their jollity. A few felected favourites were kept to fupper; amongft thefe *Bancho* and his fifter, who having got notice by the phyfician that young *Fleans* had gone to reft, quite compofed, they could not refift *Macbeth's* importunities to fleep in the palace.

‘ Now the hour arriving for the accomplifhment of the Queen's inhuman purpofes, fhe retired with the devoted *Inetta*, and another, a lady of the *Broad Albane* family, a maid of honour, to their refpective apartments. Soon afterwards *Macbeth* conducts *Bancho* into the bed-chamber, allotted for him, but which for the fore part of that night was to be occupied by *Macbeth*; it was the next adjoining to the Queen's; here they both undrefs, and in their loofe night gowns, *Macbeth* leads *Bancho* into his wife's room, where every thing appeared as if prepared for the reception

Q 2   of

of a bridegroom : how foon *Bancho* was ready to ftep into bed, he drew afide the curtains on purpofe that the Queen might fee him, fo as not to be deceived in the perfon intended to fill her arms ; and thereupon *Macbeth* withdrew.

'*Bancho*, rather feduced, than tempted to this trial of his manhood, lay a few minutes infenfible to any of thofe emotions, which men are apt to feel when they get within the curtains, to a new object of their own courting ; but at length the communicative warmth, which feldom fails to move perfons of a different fex, when in one bed, began to quicken in the deftined victim; and turning himfelf to the clofer embrace, horrid to relate ! fhe received him on the point of a dagger fhe had fecreted in the bed for the purpofe, and which fhe barbaroufly thruft home to his heart !

' We muft next follow *Macbeth* to the commiffion of an action on his part, no otherwife lefs flagitious than his wife's, than that the temptation to it was not quite fo diabolical. He no fooner had bid good night to *Bancho*, than he haftened to the apartment of the fifter of *Broad Albane*, who had been corrupted to facilitate the ruin of the lovely *Inetta*; and having learnt from her, that the unfufpicious charmer, had

had been prevailed upon to swallow the opiate cordial prepared for her, he might certainly enter into the folds of ravishment, without alarming her. The devoted sacrifice slept in the next room; and slept so profoundly, that the betrayer had an opportunity unobstructed, of feasting his greedy eyes, and sacrilegious hands, with every excitement to lust, which a form so perfect could inflame him with! until by every nerve being overcharged with swelling emotions, and impatient for gratification, he like a thief purloined uncomplete fruition! insensible as she was, such unusual disturbance and painful agitation awoke her; but no words, not even can imagination form an adequate idea of the agonies which distracted her, how soon she became conscious of her situation! And yet the unpitying wretch, unmoved by such immense distress, conceiving, that now reanimated, she might yet bestow more perfect bliss, again essays to aggravate the mighty woe, by forcing her to feel, in feeble struggling a repetition of the ill, which, already, she had insensibly submitted to! At length, alarmed with uncouth distant shrieks, he left the pitiable object, to the relief of death, or to the less supportable wailings of plundered innocence!

O 3 The

' The inhuman Queen had no sooner finished the murder of *Bancho*, than she jumped from the bed and screamed out so vehemently, that she soon aroused the neighbouring ladies of her bed-chamber, and even the more remote guards ; she counterfeited a fort of distraction to a nicety, and in that consternation the King entered, while madam was pouring forth invectives against the lifeless *Bancho*, for having made a daring attempt to rob her of her virtue, and to dishonour the King's bed ; which nothing, she said, could have prevented, but by a seeming compliance, to wait the opportunity of his laying aside the dagger which he had held drawn at her bosom, quickly to snatch it up, and instantly to plunge it into his ! She dissembled this affair so well, that she had already gained over both the attendants and guards into a belief of the fact, as she related it. *Macbeth* however pretended not only the last surprize, but appeared as if extremely unwilling to credit such an imputation against his cousin *Bancho* ; he ordered that a council should be called to meet within three hours; that the Queen, with all those persons who at first were witnesses of the situation, should attend ; for that in a question where the parties were so nearly connected with him, he would not trust himself felf as judge, but leave it to the more impartial inquiry of a council.

'In the mean time he returned to the chamber in which he had locked up the wretched *Inetta*; fhe had now recovered fome fenfe of her lamentable condition, and at fight of him fhe fent forth fuch a difmal fhriek, as even ftruck his own hardened foul with terror! he prayed that for her own fake fhe would be patient for a moment, vowed that the ardour of his paffion, and the coldnefs with which fhe had treated him, urged him to commit what he had done, and what his own confcience blamed him for: But be not fo much furprifed, my dear *Inetta*, continued he; your virtuous brother *Bancbo!* had this fame night the like defign againft the honour of the Queen; and which nothing could have prevented the perpetration of, but that fhe having more the foul of a man, than of a woman, had refolution, by means of his own dagger, to protect her perfon and my honour from the meditated affault! Such, fuch, fays he, is the irrefiftable power of real love, that it will break through every barrier of obftruction! Reconcile yourfelf then, thou lovelieft of thy fex, to what is paft; my whole life fhall be fpent in making you reparation for what you have fuffered; and if you can

act

act with prudence, even the half of my
crown may not be without your reach!
in vain did she often attempt to interrupt
him, his very voice founding in her ears
worse than the hifs of ferpents! But catch-
ing at his last words, Impious wretch!
said she indignantly, and dost thou think
as bafely of my virtue as of thy own! that
thou couldst repair thy treachery to me
by perfidy to thy Queen!—Be gone! let me
escape from this manfion of devils, that
after exhaufting the remaining ftrength you
have left me, in invocations to heaven and
earth for vengeance, I may next bury my
diftrefs in the unreproaching grave!
Soothing being vain, he next reforts to
threats; and telling her, that she, her
nephew, and whole family, being in his
power, if she perfifted in her obftinacy, nay,
if she would not promife fecrecy, he would
make a fatal facrifice of every one of them
to his provoked refentment. Never was unhappy woman fo perplexed; she promifed
and unpromifed in the fame inftant, but
at laft imploring on her knees permiffion to
inquire after her nephew's health, and pro-
mifing to admit him to her own apartment
in the afternoon, he gave her leave to retire.

'The Council was now met, to hear and
judge of the information concerning *Ban-*
cho's.

cho's plot upon the Queen, and the caufe of his fudden death. The artful Queen had every point of evidence quite clear, *Bancho*'s undrefs, his body being actually found in her bed, her loud and diftracted fcreams, the diftrefs and confufion in which fhe at firft appeared; in fhort every prefumption concurred to exculpate her, and condemn the unhappy *Bancho!* I alone doubted; I defired that the fatal poinard fhould be openly expofed; perhaps fome one might inform, if ever, and where it had been feen before; becaufe fure I faid it was none of *Bancho*'s; in that moment I ftood fingle, even the penetrating *Argyle*, till after he had feen *Inetta*, was unfufpicious: and in fine, this dark affair was fo well conducted on the part of *Macbeth* and his wife, that the majority of the council would have voted fome fort of ignominy upon the dead body; but *Macbeth*, who until the laft, had fat filent, as if determined that his opinion, or what he fhould fay, might biafs no mortal, then rofe up and fpoke; he pathetically regreted, that by fuch an unexpected degeneracy in the breaft of his coufin *Bancho*, he had fuffered, as well as the ftate, an irreparable lofs; the ftate had loft a good foldier and a counfellor; he had, for his fhare, not only loft thefe, but withal, the

partner

partner of his foul, his firft confident, and fincere friend! He thank'd the council for the refentment they were willing to fhew to the indignity offered to his honour ; but hoped, as the injury was pointed chiefly againft himfelf, they would allow him to difpenfe with any mark of infamy intended to be done upon the corpfe, and permit that it might be decently interred : This well affected clemency, had any fufpicions got place, would have gone fome length to banifh them, for it wrought greatly in *Macbeth*'s favour.

'How foon the Council rofe, the noble *Argyle* who was a near relation to the mother of *Inetta*, went directly to *Bancho*'s houfe in order to carry condolence to his fon and fifter : The melancholy *Inetta* had fhut herfelf up to ruminate over her diftrefsful condition ; having ordered admittance to be refufed to every body, excepting only *Argyle*, to whom fhe was refolved fully to unbofom herfelf; fhe did fo accordingly ; but it is impoffible to give you any fort of copy of the original defcription which the venerable *Argyle* gave me of the affecting picture he beheld in the dejected, defponding *Inetta!* He then arranged every circumftance relating to the two families fince the hour of *Macbeth*'s firft declaration of love to *Inetta* ; and from the whole

he

he concluded that *Macbeth* and his wife had actually commited thefe execrable villanies now related of them. The firft ftep he took, was immediately to remove *Fleans* into *England*; and then by degrees to imprefs the minds of all thofe whom he could perfuade into confidence with him, with his own fentiments of the murder,, and to wait patiently for that hour when they fhould have ftrength fufficient, to do juftice to the blood and honour of *Bancho*'s family. But fo uncommonly popular had *Macbeth* by this time rendered himfelf, that almoft every body were fpies for him; I knew this better than any body elfe; and although from *Argyle*'s relation to me of what he had been informed by *Inetta*, I was equally impreffed with fufpicions; yet I ftill recommended to *Argyle* the utmoft circumfpection in his conduct; and what has made you, *Glamis*, as well as many of the nobility of thefe days, entertain jealoufies with regard to me? it was becaufe I would never declare my fentiments in the prefence of any mortal, where there could be a poffibility of conveying them to the ear of the King.

'Sufpicions of the foul play which *Bancho* and his fifter had fuffered, gained ground every day; and many of the moft virtuous of the nobles having withdrawn
their

their attendance from court, awakened fearful apprehenfions in the King, who had, by corrupting their domefticks and others who had beft accefs to their privacies, procured intelligence of almoft every converfation they held. He iffued a proclamation requiring their attendance, on pretence of affifting in the affairs of government; a few appeared, but many more excufed themfelves and continued in retirement: at length he difpatched public meffengers with armed force, to apprehend thofe againft whom he had the cleareft proofs of having fcandalized him; and as many as were found out, were brought to *Perth*, where they underwent a form of trial, were convicted of difobedience, of undutiful and feditious difcourfe, and capitally condemned. Some days previous to their execution, I took an opportunity to expoftulate with him upon the feverity of the meafures he was purfuing; he turned fhort upon me; ha! faid he, is it fo, and is *Angus* alfo my enemy? that is more than I feared! but know, Thane! that as there is no other choice left me, but either to fall myfelf, or to rid the kingdom of thofe fecret enemies who are daily forming cabals againft me, I am refolved to finifh my work, and not be the tame dependant upon their fmiles or frowns that my

predeceffor

predecessor was! you know, continued he, a great deal of the late undermining schemes, but notwithstanding all the confidence I have placed in you, you luckily know not half that I know: and let me advise, that for the future, even *Angus* be cautious how he speaks and acts; it would be with reluctance I should also punish him: so saying, he left me to chew the cud upon what I had heard; and I confess, that for my own safety, and that I might have any power at all left me to be useful, I thereafter dissembled a conformity to his ways of proceeding, howsoever absurd; resolving to wait until an opportunity should present itself, when I might openly act more consistently with my own sentiments.

' The first trial he made, whether or no I was sincere in the approbation of his arbitrary schemes, was to require my signature to an act of forfeiture against the noble Thane of *Argyle*, who had hitherto baffled every inquiry for discovering his haunts: he knew there was the strictest amity between the Thane and me, and he therefore expected, that I would for certain remonstrate against a proceeding so affecting to myself; but I was prepared for him; and after subscribing to the forfeiture with the utmost seeming readiness, I informed him of what, however, he had intelligence of

P   by

by other means ; that I knew that *Argyle*'s
son, the young *Lorn*, was privately entertained at an aunt's houfe, not very remote;
and I advifed, that *Lorn* fhould be forth-
with taken into cuftody, and then a frefh
proclamation iffued, that unlefs *Argyle*,
within a fixed time, did furrender, and
anfwer to his accufation, that his fon fhould,
at the expiration of the fummons, be made
a public facrifice! This propofition he
greedily approved, and I thereby had the
good fortune to re-eftablifh myfelf in his
confidence. *Lorn* was immediately feized
upon, and according to my wifh, was
committed into my cuftody. The pious
father, in confequence, furrendered in a few
days thereafter. The King, after having
examined him himfelf, and endeavouring
in vain to pump out of him a full difcovery
of the fecret purpofes of his enemies, recommended a fecond examination by me,
hoping, that through the power of that
friendfhip that had long fubfifted between.
us, I might draw from him, in confidence,
a difcovery which the King could not effect.
I undertook the tafk; but gueffing that the
King would conceal himfelf, fo as to be
within hearing, I managed the conference
fo dextroufly, that while I gained upon
Macbeth's opinion of my fidelity to him, I
ftirred up the higheft indignation againft
me

me in the breaſt of honeſt *Argyle.* After
this examination was over, *Macbeth,* who
knew as well as myſelf all that had paſſed,
ſhewed, however, a plauſible impatience to
get the account of it from me; I related it
as it was; told him, I could as yet learn
nothing new from him; that he acknowledged an inſuperable averſion to the King,
and no leſs to myſelf; and that, finally, he
had declared, that the offer of no rewards,
nor the fear of any puniſhment, ſhould ever
prevail with him to attach himſelf to a man
who had contrived the murder of one couſin,
and committed a barbarous rape upon the
perſon of another, which the unfortunate
Inetta, now languiſhing in a monaſtery,
declared, with inconteſtable proofs, to all
the world! The enraged *Macbeth* propoſed
inſtantly to condemn him to the torture,
which I affected at once to concur in, and
I actually gave orders to prepare for it;
but in the interim, throwing myſelf, as if
by accident, in the King's way, I began to
reaſon with him upon the affair of *Argyle.*
I told him, that there was no doubt but it
was in *Argyle's* power to make diſcoveries
of the higheſt importance, but that I knew
him to poſſeſs a firmneſs of ſoul not to be
ſhaken by the moſt excruciating torments!
That, of all the nobles, he was undoubtedly
the moſt popular; and that however much

it

it might be in our powers by force to over-
awe the immediate refentments of the
people, yet the public torture and execution of one fo much their idol, would take
fuch root in their minds, as might burft out
upon fome occafion, when leaft expected.
I concluded, by affirming, that for certain,
if for nothing elfe but his obftinacy, when
his Majefty had made him a tender of
mercy, he richly deferved death; but in-
finuating, that if I had fome lefs formal
opportunities of entering into converfation
with him, and of impreffing upon his mind
a revival of our ancient friendfhip, I flattered myfelf I might ftill work fomething
out of him; that if, in the end, I fhould
find all my addrefs in vain, I, in that cafe,
fubmitted it, whether it would not be more
eligible to make away with him in a private
manner, rather than to increafe the grumblings of the people, by making him a public
example: nay, I further told him, that if
he would leave it to my management, I
would conduct it fo, as to turn the voice of
popularity for the King, and againft *Argyle*;
for by committing him to my keeping,
whom the world believed to be his friend,
and engaging to anfwer for the confequences
with my own life, I argued, that the public
would, in the firft place, applaud the King's
lenity; and when it fhould be judged neceffary

ceffary to difpatch him, (for I infifted that
it would be dangerous to let him live) that
I would however contrive it fo, that every
body fhould believe he had deftroyed himfelf.

‘ The King gave an ear to this reafoning ; and after he had communicated it to
the Queen, who alfo approved, and both
being happy to think of my voluntarily
taking fo large a fhare of guilt upon myfelf, it was agreed that *Argyle* fhould be left
entirely at my difpofal : I therefore went in
perfon, and enlarged him from his prifon ;
and conducted him openly, and without
any guard, to my own houfe ; however, he
paffed through the approving populace
with a fullennefs that ftill fpoke difcontent.
I took the firft opportunity of difclofing
my real fentiments to *Argyle* ; prayed him
to forget the behaviour with which I carried myfelf to him in the beginning, and
convinced him of the neceffity I lay under
of acting as I did, becaufe I was certain we
were then in the hearing of *Macbeth* ; but
that it then was, as it ftill was, my intention, not only to fave his life, but to render him and his family every poffible fervice.
The Thane gazed upon me, fufpicious !
but that fincere uniformity which he read
in the compofure of my countenance, being
more fatisfying to him than words, he embraced

braced me, and said he should be at my
disposal. I told him, that his destruction
had been resolved upon, not only by death,
but by torture; and that, if possible, to
prevent either the one or the other, I had
myself undertaken to have him privately
murdered, to the end, that at the same
time that *Macbeth*'s apprehensions of danger from his influence might be at an end,
the fury of his friends might not be provoked by the sight of a public execution:
that, in consistency with my project, I would
contrive means for his escape, on condition,
(for I could not be safe myself upon any
other) that he would submit, until better
times should relieve him, to a confinement
in my castle at *Ila*; and that I should, by a
management in this sort, have it still in my
power to protect and rear up his son, whose
existence would be less alarming, when it
was believed the father was actually dead.
To all which the worthy Thane, yet eager
on revenge, reluctantly assented. *Argyle*
had one servant, in whom he could confide,
and I selected one of the most trusty of my
own, to accomplish the execution of so important a design; these I employed, in the
uniform of guards, to bring from prison a
malefactor, then under sentence of death,
to my house; the servants strangled him,
stript him, and put upon him the clothes
of

of the Thane, who, attended only by my
fervant, I fent off in difguife the fame night.
The malefactor was much of the fame fta-
ture with *Argyle*; fo that having, after his
death, ordered his face to be mangled, I
next morning waited on *Macbeth*; and telling him, that after ufing every artifice in
my power to make the flubborn Thane
fpeak out, all had been to no purpofe: I
even faid, that I had at firft but partly
ftrangled him, and then relieved him, juft
upon the edge of death, but nothing could
prevail, till at length I was provoked beyond meafure, and had finifhed him, with
only one fervant in the fecret, who was prepared to affert with me, that he had cut his
own throat. The King applauded what
had been done; but anxious, as I expected,
to be convinced of the fact, he accompanied
me home, where he gratified his inhuman
eyes with the miferable fpectacle: he then
cordially embraced me, and faid, I had indeed proved myfelf his friend! The Court
affected to lament the cataftrophe; the
King's own family went into mourning,
and the body was ordered private, but de-
cent burial.——This, my dear *Lorn*, is the
greateft debt you owe me; thy noble father
yet lives, unknown to you, to *Eugenia*, or
to any other mortal, but the faithful fervant who lives with him! and how foon we
can

can find a veffel to proceed to *Fla*, we may
all have the happinefs, with himfelf, of
felicitating one another in the reftoration
of one of the beft of men !

' *Lorn* was ftruck with unutterable joy,
in the hopes of one day embracing that
author of his being, whom he had for fo
long a time imagined had no exiftence !
The venerable *Glamis*, as if enchanted, expreffed a gladnefs through every ftriking
feature ! Now *Angus*, faid he, you have by
this one mafterly ftroke of management
wafhed clean every imputed ftain from
thy adminiftration ! and at this moment I
find myfelf as prone to interpret with fa-
vourablenefs, every tranfaction of your
miniftry, as before I ftigmatized them as
infamous and diabolical ! and, now, my
dear friend, added he, proceed in your relation ; until now, I liftened to you with
fufpicious attention ; to the fequel, I fhall
hear you with confidence and pleafure.

' This fuppofed deftruction of *Argyle*,
continued *Angus*, fixed me fo firmly in the
good graces of the tyrant (for fuch was
he now become) that every diffidence of
me was banifhed ; and it was by that
means that young *Lorn* was fo abfolutely
left in my direction ; I promifed to *Macbeth* that I would train him up in fuch principles, as fhould be the moft agreeable to
his.

his inclinations, and thereby fecure not only himfelf, but the powerful connections of his family in the court intereft : to which end I propofed, to prevent his being expofed to the defigning feduction of others, to confine him as a fort of ftate prifoner to the boundaries of my own houfe, until he fhall arrive to fuch an age as fhould entitle him to the King's particular notice ; and that then the enlargement fhould appear to him to be the effect of royal favour : And it was purely that I might act fo confiftently with thefe engagements of good policy, as not to be liable to any fufpicions of meaning otherwife, that made my entertainment of *Lorn* bear fo much the appearance of an imprifonment.

' However, the number of the late mercilefs executions, joined to other apprehenfions and jealoufies, difpofed every nobleman and gentleman, who could do it with decency, to withdraw themfelves from the court ; fo that in a little time there were none to be feen about it but a band of fycophants and cut-throats, who were ready not only to approve, but to execute, the moft arbitrary meafures, that the moft barbarous of Kings had a heart to contrive. By their means, and the inftigations of the Queen, there was nothing to be heard of but

but daily proclamations of attainder and forfeiture. The wifeft heads, the beft hearts, and nobleft blood of the nation, muft all be perfecuted, to make vacant places of honour, power and truft, for the moft confummate ruffians, that any nation ever produced; thefe, by gratifying every promptitude to luft in their fovereign tyrant, might themfelves commit, with impunity, every degree of outrage, robbery and rapine they had a mind to ; which if you will give me leave, I fhall illuftrate by one fhocking example.

' There was a gentleman of family in the highlands, named *Maclean*; he had a moft beautiful wife with whom he had lived, and was living, in a ftate of the utmoft concord and felicity ; one of *Macbeth*'s body guards happening to ride paft the caftle of *Maclean*, faw his wife, and immediately conceived a defire to enjoy her; he returned to the caftle, and after being entertained with every proof of hofpitality, he had the impudence in the hufbands prefence to offer unbecoming addreffes to the wife of *Maclean*, which he enforced by the argument of his influence at court, and his being fo much a favourite with the King, that he was employed in all his moft fecret and perfonal expeditions ; the hufband and wife both treated fuch an infult with the contempt

contempt it deferved : *Maclean* ordered
him to quit his houfe in an inftant, or
fwore he would immediately fend his head
as a prefent to his King, with a label intimating the daring affront he had offered to
his family. The monfter thought it beft to
obey, and thanklefsly left his entertainers,
with a heart as full of refentment as of luft:
From the caftle he went immediately in
queft of fome of his profligate brethren,
and having found out four or five as big
ruffians as himfelf, he with them, returns
to the caftle in the dead of night ; and
after fetting fire to one part of it, they entered fword in hand into another: *Maclean*
did not dream of his ungrateful gueft, but
fufpecting them to be a party authorifed by
the King to apprehend and carry him off
a prifoner, on account of a backwardnefs
he had fhewn to deliver up fome rights of
vaffalage, then in his poffeffion ; he endeavoured to conceal himfelf and the unhappy wife imagining fhe rifked nothing,
affifted in leting him down from a back
window from which he might make his efcape. She had juft returned, and was
making towards her own chamber, when
the villain who had infulted her at mid-day,
caught her rudely in his arms ; and fuppofing that *Maclean* was ftill in his chamber, he locked the door, and fet fire to it !
he

he next ordered his emissaries to bring off
the children, and thus they forcibly carried away the unhappy mother and three
infants, leaving the house in a blaze,
and dragging them about the distance
of a mile or two to the cottage of one of
the ravagers confederates ; where the first
ruffian insisted that the the poor helpless
lady, should unresistingly submit to gratify his foul desire, or that instant see her
innocent babes butchered before her eyes !
Prayers, tears and struggling were all use-
less : Life just supported her to behold one
of the ruffians massacre one of the
children! She then fainted away, and between the agonies of life and death, the
villian not only perpetrated a most brutal
ravishment, but had the still more unexampled barbarity, to suffer his vile accom-
plices to commit the same execrable action.
In the mean time *Maclean* having walked
round his house, having seen part of it on
fire, and observing no guards about it,
supposed then, that the alarm had been
rather from thieves, than from troops ; he
re-entered his house, but seeing no body
but two or three servants running wildly
to and fro in search of him and his wife,
of whom, with his children, he found he
had been rob'd ; he was, you may believe, in a state of the utmost distraction !
How

How soon the ruffians had finished their savage purpose, they went their ways, leaving the poor abused gentlewoman, deprived of all sensation, besmeared with the blood of one, and amidst the heart-rending cries of the two surviving children! In this deplorable condition, did the miserable husband, after some hours search, find his violated family! What could be done in such a case for her recovery, was done but ineffectually; the poor woman did not survive the calamity many hours.

'Maclean then fearless, or rather careless of the King's resentment, presents himself at court, and supplicates redress. The villain owned the flagitious fact, but urged in his defence, that it was *in terrorem* of others, who disputed the King's authority; and having appealed to the false testimony of his accessaries, *Maclean* was accused of having spoken contemptuously of the King; and in fine, in place of obtaining redress, he was thrown into prison, and there secretly murdered.

'It would be too shocking to the humane ear, if I should recount any more of the barbarities, with which every day then distinguished this flagitious reign! I dissembled almost a constant indisposition, that I might shun the mortification of being present in such a diabolical council,

Q which

which was then compofed of fuch monfters
only, as could be moft forward in contriving
and executing the deftruction of thofe of
their fellow creatures whofe power or virtues rendered them fufpected by, and obnoxious to the tyrant. And I, may with
truth affure you, that even I, who ftill
held the nominal, without any fhare of the
executive office of a minifter, feldom went
to fleep, that I did not dread the being
furprifed, with my family, by affaffins, before next morning. So that however flattering the grandeur of a prime minifter
may be, it is for the moft part a fituation rather to be pitied than envied. If a
weak King is on the throne, you are fure
to be perplexed with the dangerous emula-
tion of factions ; and if a tyrant reigns,
you muft give the fanction of your name
to deeds horrible to think of ; and the ra-
rity of a fovereign untinctured with neither
the one nor the other, gives the chance a-
gainft any well meaning minifter, whether
his ftation is to be defireable or not:
people who have no accefs to penetrate into
the fecret machinery of government, often
blame the minifter with mifmanagements,
which are purely the effects of either the
weak or defpotick temper of the monarch,
whofe blemifhes it is at the fame time his
favourites duty to throw a veil over, if in
                                    his

His power. This was a duty which I con-
fels I perfevered in too long, until at length
I found myfelf in a dilemma, out of which
I could hardly hope to extricate myfelf.

It would fpin out my relation to too great
a length, otherwife I fhould now give you
fome account in what manner the young
Lorn was educated, and paft his time during
the apparent confinement under which he
continued in my guardianfhip ; and of the
progrefs of an intimacy, a friendfhip, and
at laft the generous paffion which mutually
glowed in his, and the breaft of my *Eugenia* ; but my fpirits are already too much
exhaufted to fupport me through that affecting detail : I will therefore leave the dif-
cuffion of that interefting part of the memoirs of thefe days to *Lorn* himfelf, who
will be capable of relating it the more emphatically, that he will not fpeak from information only, but from feelings. I fhall
therefore conclude this tedious narration by
one other fatal proof of the tyrant's cruelty,
which will be the more neceffary, that the
unhappy fufferer by it, being now in
England, and a nobleman not only of
great power and property, but of as active
a fpirit as any man of the country he has
fled from ; it fhall foon be my bufinefs to
find him out, that together with him, and
the other exiles, meafures may be concerted

certed, for fupplicating the aid of the *Englifh*, and with their generous affiftance to endeavour the redemption of our bleeding country.

' Although the *Queen*'s arbitary and inhuman temper continued ftill impenetrable to the awakenings of confcience, it was not now fo with *Macbeth*; he was afraid of every moving figure that came near him! he ftarted at every noife! in fhort, he was afraid of himfelf! Thefe admonitions of a guilty confcience put him in the mind of erecting fome ftrong hold for his perfonal fecurity, and it was therefore that he founded that ftrong fortification on the top of *Dunfinane* hill, to the building of which he commanded by proclamation that every nobleman and gentleman in the kingdom fhould contribute, by furnifhing money, materials, and artificers, in proportion to the extent of their feveral eftates. At this time *Macduff*, the noble Thane of *Fife*, whofe power and virtue had already rendered him odious to the iniquitous court, became the next great object of the King and Queen's refentment; he could not prevail with himfelf to harrafs his tenants and vaffals by giving obedience to the King's proclamation; he therefore dreaded juftly the effects of his refentment, and happily for him made his efcape into *England*, leaving

ing the management of all his affairs entirely to his lady, who being nearly related
to *Macbeth*, he flattered himself, might
elude every bad consequence of his wrath.
Macbeth suspecting that *Macduff* would
meditate an escape, summoned some of his
chosen banditti, and putting himself at
their head, marched, so soon as the days of
the proclamations had expired, with great
privacy towards the estate of *Macduff*, with
a view to seize his person and to plunder
his possessions. He arrived in the night, and
surrounded *Macduff*'s castle, and being permitted to enter without any sort of resistance, the alarmed lady flung herself,
with her innocent crying children, pro-
strate before him, imploring for mercy.
His fierce soul was now agitated with jarring passions! he was furious on account
of *Macduff*'s escape; while at the same
time the beautiful figure of lady *Macduff*,
greatly heightened by the supplicating posture into which she had thrown herself,
touched his rapacious heart with a different emotion! At first he dissembled a gentleness now become unnatural to him; he
raised her up, and embracing her with the
warmth rather of authority than complacency, she shook with terrour! he immediately told her with an abruptness,
shocking to innocence, that she had one

Q 3   way,

way, and but one left, to save the lives of her children, and her husband's possessions; and that was, to comply instantly, and gratify the passion she had kindled in him! She kneeled! she teared! she expostulated with all the energy of afflictive sensation! It was all in vain! In vain did she plead her admitting him into the castle as a relation, as her friend, and as her King! in vain did she urge every abuse of hospitality, and the unkingly manner by which he offered to violate its laws. In fine, having assumed a firmness which ever accompanies determined virtue, she told him she valued her fortune, she loved her children, and she revered her husband, and yet, bid him know that she prefered her honour to all! The unfeeling tyrant laughed in ridicule, ordered her two children to be murdered in her eye sight, and then commanding that she should be bound and carried into her bed-chamber! he followed, and there, after having committed the most execrable ravishment that ever man but himself could dare the commission of, that he might put an end to her agonized groans, he also ordered herself to be murdered! He next proclamed *Macduff* a traitor, forfeited his estates, and prohibited correspondence with him on pain of death and confiscation!

On

' On his return from this scene of barbarity, he came on a visit to my house, on purpose to learn how such transactions were relished by me ; and most unfortunately, though considering that it has produced this happy escape, I may rather say fortunately, he cast his eye, for the first time since she had arrived at the state of puberty, upon my *Eugenia*, whom, until that hour, I had carefully concealed from his rapacious eyes ; he catched fire at sight of her beauty, and even in the instant made insinuations against her virtue ! Nay he had the effrontery to demand her of myself, for his mistress! the dreadful examples of *Inetta* and *Bancho* were too full in my memory, not to caution me against the effects of a flat denial ; on the contrary, I tried only to defer the shocking purpose, by promising that I would myself recommend his suit, and exhort her to a sensibility of the preference with which he considered her. By this means I flattered myself with gaining some days, and was in the mean time busy meditating the most probable measures for an escape. *Eugenia*, who was not altogether a stranger to the vicious dispositions of *Macbeth*, became miserable with fear, since the first approach he made to her ; he made his errands more frequent at my house, and it was with the utmost difficulty that

the

the terrified *Eugenia* could avoid his addresses ; it was her custom, how soon she had heard of his visit, to retire to some unfrequented place in the gardens : at length he grew very impatient, and one day having flatly accused me with at least a tepidity in his service, if not a full intention to deceive him, he peremptorily demanded to see her ; I trembled for the consequence, and endeavoured once more to divert him from the purpose, by assuring him, that I had already opened the subject to her ; and hoped, that by a conference or two more, I should be able to conquer her objections, and to reconcile her to the honour he intended for her ; but that, as no such view had ever before entered into either her's or my head ; and that, as every lesson she had studied from her infancy, having been, without regarding distinctions of men, totally repugnant to the thoughts of any pleasure or grandeur not consistent with virtue, a little time was necessary to reason her into an alteration of her sentiments ; for I told him, it would indeed be a hardship put upon me, to command by authority what I hoped so soon to accomplish by persuasion. He appeared somewhat satisfied, but persisted in seeing her, promising at the same time, on his word, that he should be so far from offering any thing that might disgust her,

her, that on that occasion he would only mention love with great delicateness. To please him, I went out to call her, but finding she was not in the house, I walked with him into the garden ; and after a variety of turns, we at last discovered her very serious with young *Lorn* ; at sight of whom the King fell into a most violent fury: What, says he, do you nurse up that young rebel, who breathes only by my indulgence, to be a bar to my enjoyments? 'Tis enough ; I will soon put an end to that rivalship : So saying, he flung out of the garden with such aggravation in every feature, as sufficiently indicated, that the execution of some dreadful purpose would soon follow. He immediately set guard upon my house ; so that I now seeing we had not a moment to lose, I made fast every gate and door; and retiring, with *Lorn* and *Eugenia*, to the most detached part of the house, and having filled our pockets with as much gold, and as many jewels as we could carry, we let ourselves down by a stool, flung conveniently with ropes, from a back window, from whence, unseen and unsuspected, we could get into a stable-yard ; and thence, with one trusty servant only, taking four of my best horses, we rode, with all haste, towards the Highlands. As the servant was well acquainted through the muirs, and

night

night coming on, it was impoffible to trace us. We had rode, at full fpeed, for almoft fix hours, without a halt, until the unufual fatigue having quite overcome the tender *Eugenia*, and there being no fort of habitation within our view, we were fain to form in the heath the beft beds we could; and there we embraced a very refrefhing repofe, being affured by the fervant, that we were at leaft thirty miles diftant from *Perth*, and by fuch an unfrequented road, that we had nothing to apprehend from a purfuit. Having here, without fleeping, repofed ourfelves about three hours, we were anxious to proceed; but the horfes, no lefs fatigued than their riders, and having no other nourifhment than they could glean amongft the bufhes, were all unfit for fervice, except the one that I had rid: upon that one therefore we mounted the fervant, and fent him forward to difcover any fort of dwelling, whilft we trudged after him as well as we could, leading our beafts. We had not however walked above three hours, when we defcried the fervant returning towards us with frefh horfes, accompanied by their mafter, a vaffal to *Cummin* the Thane of *Badenoch*, who being at that time a minor, had efcaped the notice of *Macbeth*. Here we met with a very hofpitable reception; but withal, were advifed not to tarry long

in

in the fame place, as there were but few
days paffed, but fome or other of the court
fpies were traverfing the country.

' We continued our flight the next and
following day, and then made towards the
Mull of *Galloway*; and, as Providence
kindly ordered it, we had juft got on board
our fmall bark when the Tyrant's purfuers
arrived on the beach, and, in our fight,
feized our horfes, and, to the forrow of us
all, the faithful fervant who had been fo
ufeful in our efcape. We fet fail immediately, intending to fteer firft for *Ifla*, in
order to make the noble Thane of *Argyle*
a partner in our efcape; but the wind not
ferving, and ftill fearing to be chaced, we
were obliged to obey the winds, and to
make for the *Englifh* coaft directly. Nothing extraordinary happened in our paffage,
until we came within fight of this friendly
fhore, where we have enjoyed a fympathy
and protection equal to the noblenefs of
thofe fouls which beftow it.'

Angus having thus finifhed his narration,
the venerable *Glamis* embraced him in tears
of reconciliation, fadly interrupted with the
fwelling fighs which rofe upon the thoughts
of his diftreffed country. The generous
heart of *Edmund*, and the others prefent,
were

were proportionably moved ; and the whole concluded, not only in prayers, but in firm refolves, to leave nothing undone for the recovery of the honour and rights of that oppreffed kingdom.

We have already feen to what accident it was owing, that the young *Lorn,* when no more than thirteen years of age, came into the hands of *Angus* ; but his entertainment, and the manner of his education, with a variety of circumftances, both inftructing and interefting, during his nurture and tutelage in that family, remains to be related ; a tafk, as our manufcript informs, which was performed by himfelf, to gratify the anxious inclinations of his generous benefactors.

This fmall, but happy fociety, having next day conveened in *Edmund's* garden, when the feafonable ferenity of a delightful day contributed to heighten the attention fuitable to fuch an affecting narration, *Lorn* thus proceeded :

‘ You have heard, faid he, by what means the Tyrant deftined me to confinement ; how difficult then muft it be for me to do juftice to that benignity, which, in place of a prifon, had prepared for me an academy ; for I had been but a few days
under

under the hofpitable roof of the noble *Angus*, till I found myfelf in the hands of preceptors, well chofen, not to inftruct me fimply in the knowledge of languages and fciences, but to form my mind to the moft genuine notions of virtue and philofophy; and in place of being trained, agreeable to the bafe purpofe of *Macbeth*, to a tame fubjection to meafures of flavery and oppreffion, my leffons were fuch as infpired me continually with an abhorrence of fuch fatal doctrines.

' That affiduity and pleafure with which I applied myfelf to ftudy, and the paternal fympathy of my guardian, left me no room to imagine I was in confinement; and as in intervals I had opportunities of relaxing my mind with the engaging prattle of the little charming *Eugenia*, then but ten years old, my time was unencumbered with any fort of heavinefs. We were then both too young to be fufceptible of amorous impreffions; yet in that, the very dawn of her beauties, there was a fomething that foretold my future enjoyments. It is with pleafure I do, even now, recollect that eagernefs, with which, in the beginning of defires to be agreeable to each other, we haftened to meet our dancing mafter in the hall, where a mutual difpofition to pleafe, promoted greatly the perfection to which we foon ar-

R   rived

rived in that exercise. Careful not to interrupt me, she would often steal into my study while I was under the tuition of my masters, and listen with an attention unusual at her age. Such an early tendency to acquire superior knowledge, disposed me to re-communicate to her such of my lessons as were best adapted to a female genius: I took delight in making her acquainted with every amiable character I learnt from history. I remember, that upon one occasion I was expatiating upon the different effects produced by the virtuous or vicious habits of the *Greeks* and *Romans*; at one time admiring the wisdom, prudence and humanity, of an *Augustus* or a *Vespasian*; at another, depreciating the villainy and barbarity of a *Nero*, *Caligula* and *Domitian*; when the infant charmer observed—I know not (said she) if in our days we shall ever see an *Augustus* or a *Vespasian*, but surely the actions of a *Nero* and *Caligula* are too common to us: however, (continued the surprising *Eugenia*) I have often heard my dear papa advise every one to be slow in passing judgment on the actions of others, till we can be sure that our own hearts are inclined to correct them; and that good is often produced from the consequence of the most apparent evil. This (said she) I am already convinced of, because, if I had

been

been born in a more perfect reign, you
fhould not have been confined to this houfe,
and I fhould not have had the pleafure of
fo agreeable a companion, nor of hearing
the hiftories of *thofe* fo much better times
than *thefe* we live in.

' After this manner were my juvenile
hours paffed away in reciprocal amufement
with the endearing *Eugenia*; and as fhe advanced towards the years of puberty, her
intellectuals keeping pace with the beauti-
fulnefs of her form, betokened every thing
that was lovely; and a few years gave me
fuch a forcible proof of her capacity to blefs
the object of her efteem with the moft penetrating teftimonies of exalted friendfhip,
as commanded an approbation of both fentiment and figure, that neither time nor
circumftances can ever be able to diffolve.

' There was an arbour elevated in one of
the corners of our garden, which was contrived to overlook a frequented public walk;
there, as I could, unfeen myfelf, both fee
and hear the company as they aired in this
walk, I generally diverted an hour's time
of an evening, fometimes in the defireable
converfation of my dear *Eugenia*, and fometimes alone. Upon one of my folitary
evenings, all the company having juft retired from the walk, and I ready to follow
their example, was delayed from my pur-

R 2

pofe

pofe by the voice of piercing murmurs, which feemed to force their way through moft affecting fighs : I liftened, and adhering to my ftation, foon obferved a young lady, genteelly dreffed, and of a very engaging form, place herfelf on a bench immediately under the wall contiguous to my retirement; fhe had not fat long, before fhe was joined by another more elderly gentlewoman, for whom fhe feemed to have waited. The moment the gentlewoman appeared, the fair mourner haftily demanded of her, What tidings? Is my friend at hand or not? Is he alive? The gentlewoman anfwered, Madam, be compofed, nothing bad has, I believe, yet happened, with regard to the object of your defires; my inquiries have not hitherto been complete, but I have confidents at work, who, I hope, will be able to procure us fome fatisfaction : but permit me, Madam, to afk you, how it happens, that thus dejected, you abandon the protection of your father's houfe; for without alarming you with an illgrounded diffidence, I fhould not chufe to be employed in any bufinefs that might taint my reputation? This queftion drew from the trembling *Ifabella* (fo was the lady named) a flood of tears; and how foon fhe could charge her tongue to utterance, fhe fobbed out, How hard, how cruelly hard!

is

is the fate of young women, who muft either facrifice their perfons and underftandings to the fevere opinions of unfeeling parents, or fubject their characters to unfavourable fufpicions! But, Madam, (continued fhe) you yourfelf fhall judge, from the true relation of my fad fituation, whether or no I deferve your pity and affiftance.——The condition of my father's family is not unknown to you, and therefore I need to fay nothing more on that point, than to tell you that, as a daughter of that family, I had reafon to hope for the addreffes of fuch gentlemen as fhould be able to accompany one through life with tolerable fatisfaction. Before the defections in the court of *Macbeth* arrived to fuch a pitch, that none but parafites, fycophants, and villains, were the fupporters of the throne, the accomplifhed *Killibarren*, one of the foremoft in the efteem of the late noble and worthy Thane of *Argyle*, was frequent in his vifits at my father's houfe, and a mutual approbation growing between him and me, our affections became the confequence of it. My mother, unfortunately for me, had got in her eye an old rich advocate, whom fhe intended for my hufband : this advocate was deformed in his perfon, infufferable in his humour, and covetous to the laft degree ! *Killibarren* was manly, affable, and generous ! So that it

R 3. will

will be no difficult matter to decide, which
had the preference in the heart of a young
woman juſt in the bloom of female maturity.
My father, although he had in the beginning rather given ſome countenance to the
addreſſes of *Killibarren*, was too obſequious
to the will of his wife, to oppoſe her decrees
with any degree of reſolution : ſhe accuſed
him of folly, for having hearkened to the
ſuit of a vaſſal, for a ſon-in-law, when ſhe
had it in her power to beſtow me upon a
huſband almoſt as rich, though not ſo noble,
as the Thane himſelf : in ſhort, ſhe prevailed ſo far over the good nature of my
father, that he gave me over to her diſpo-
ſal ; the conſequence of which was, that
the amiable *Killibarren* was forbid the houſe,
and I diſcharged, under the penalty of a
maternal curſe, and deprivation of fortune,
to hold any farther correſpondence with
him : but alas! the prohibition came too
late ; we had already exchanged our hearts
by reciprocal vows, too ſacred to be broken;
ſo that I found myſelf under the reluctant
neceſſity of reſorting to diſſimulation, that
I might ſhun the reſtraint of a total confinement, and be thereby deprived of the pleaſure of ſuch private interviews with my beloved, as we could procure by ſtealth. By
one artifice after another, I procraſtinated
the concluſion of affairs with *Bernard* the
advocate,

advocate, until the arrival of a circumstance
so affecting to this devotee of wealth, as at
once relieved me from his loathsome pursuits. It was just at the juncture when
Macbeth was projecting the fortification of
Dunsinane; and finding, upon examination,
that his finances were rather low at the
time, he was casting about how he might
raise a fund for that purpose, when some of
his worthy counsellors directed him to the
rich *Bernard*. *Bernard* was immediately
summoned to court, to which he had been
all his lifetime an utter stranger; he would
fain have excused his attendance, by pre-
tending indisposition; but the King instantly
ordered a detachment of his guards to fetch
him before him, dead or alive. The officer
making no sort of ceremony, entered abruptly the apartment of the advocate, and
found him earnestly occupied in disposing
his money into separate bags, for the better
concealing of it : if the indisposition of this
wretch was at first only counterfeited, it
became now indeed real : the officer secured
immediately all the money he saw, and had
it transported, alongst with its owner, to the
presence of the King. *Macbeth*, upon seeing the ghastliness which then appeared in
the advocate's figure, and the terrible tre-
mor which shook every joint of him, did
not doubt but he had been really valetudi-
nary;

nary; and at firſt aſked him, if an old man
of ſuch a feeble conſtitution was not aſhamed
to think of matrimony with a young vigorous
maid? The old miſer was not ignorant of
Macbeth's ſalacious character, and therefore the ſordid wretch, diſconcerted as he
was, bethought himſelf of throwing another
ſort of bait in the King's maw, hoping
thereby to divert his attention from a trea-
ſure more valuable to him than all the youth
and beauty on earth; he put on all the ob-
ſequiouſneſs of the vileſt pander; confeſſed
to the King, that he did intend to marry,
but with very little view to indulge any
appetite of his own; he ſaid, he had never
had the honour to be at court, becauſe he
did not know of any merit by which he
could introduce himſelf; that he had ſome-
how heard, that his Majeſty was of a very
amorous complexion; that he had for a
long while been in ſearch of a beautiful
young woman, not doubting but the illgrounded report of his wealth would render an alliance with him acceptable in moſt
families; and that it was his intention, ſo
ſoon as he could call *Iſabella* his own, to
have the honour of preſenting her to the
King, and by that means recommending
himſelf to his favour. Whether it was that
Macbeth, who was not deficient in point of
penetration, was truly ſhocked with ſuch
an

an inftance of bafenefs, as he had hardly
ever met with before; or whether it was
avidity to have the touching of the advocate's treafures, I fhall not take upon me
to determine; but juftice, for this time, exerted itfelf even in the hands of a tyrant:
he regarded the trembling *Bernard* with an
eye of piercing indignation; afked him,
how he dared to infult Majefty, by offering
to corrupt it by the moft unexamped proftitution? ordered him into immediate confinement, and proclaimed a confifcation of
all his eftate. How unfathomable are thy
ways, O Providence! Thus, from the
mouth of vice itfelf, that it might gratify
its own rapacity, was oppreffed innocence
refcued, and avarice and proftitution de-
fervedly punifhed.——But alas, Madam,
(continued *Ifabella*) my diftrefs has not
ended with the advocate's punifhment:
The no lefs abandoned, though younger,
Calendar, having hearkened attentively to
the difcourfe of *Bernard* while before the
King, became immediately a vifitor at my
father's houfe; and fo effectually gained
upon my mother, that his addreffes, ftill
more daring than the advocate's, were favoured by her: that villain *Calender*, to
whom, amongft many other barbarities, is
imputed an acceffion to the rape of *Inetta*,
and murder of her brother, as well as the
fecret

secret affaffination of the noble Thane of *Argyle*, he now perfecutes me with a proffer of his detefted heart. I have pled fo effectually with my too eafy tempered father, that I prevailed with him to reafon with my mother againft fuch a compulfion of inclination : he argued from the fatal confequences that would have attended the force fhe defigned to put upon me. by marrying me to the bafe *Bernard*; but the reputed power, intereft, and fortune of *Calender*, unhappily overbalances all the diftinguifhed merit of *Killibarren*; and I muft again be paffive under the moft difgufting importunities. The generous heart of *Killibarren*, too fenfibly touched with the mal-treatment I was forced to fubmit to, by reafon of the preference he held in my affections, has been under the moft deplorable perplexities : that cordial duty which attached him to the intereft of *Argyle*, rendered it impracticable for him to operate with his own, my relief, otherwife both of us fhould, long ere now, have embraced a voluntary banifhment, and retreated far beyond the power of a diffolute court, and the hateful perfecution of the moft infamous parafite in the whole of its circle.

When the good Thane of *Argyle*, in order to preferve the life of a fon, which was dearer to him than his own, furrendered himfelf

himself into the hands of the murderous
Tyrant, my *Killibarren*, difguifed as a woman, attended, till the Thane's fate fhould
be decided, at a cottage not far from my
father's houfe ; and it was in this delectable
retirement, known alone to the Thane and
me, where, loving and beloved, we mutually confecrated to one another thofe
vows diffolvable only by Heaven itfelf.
But alas ! thofe innocent, though ftolen,
enjoyments, were little permanent ; the
Thane was treacheroufly murdered ; the
cottage, as well as every other corner of
the country, was rummaged for his adherents ; the dear poffeffor of my heart difappeared ; I counted him dead, was feized
with a languifhment which threatened to
put a fpeedy period to my fad exiftence,
which nothing elfe could have fuftained,
but that I was thereby freed from the pur-
fuits of the fo much abhorred *Calender*.
You know, Madam, (continued the dif-
confolate *Ifabella*) how long, and how
doubtfully for life or death, I lingered under a confumfng illnefs ; but fome weeks
ago, a dawn of unexpected hope reanimated
my decaying fpirits ; the cottager's daughter, who now and then watched in my fick-
nefs, being one day habited in part of the
apparrel which difguifed the unfortunate
Killibarren, accidentally pulling from one
of

of the pockets a round piece of flate, I imagined I obferved fome characters upon it; I afked her what it was, and defired her to fhew it me; fhe told me fhe knew not what it was, fhe had found it in the pocket after the gentleman, who paffed for a woman at their hut, was gone, and that fhe had kept it ever fince; fhe gave it me, and a precious jewel it was; See here, fays fhe, taking it from her fnowy bofom, you can trace the gravings of " *Ifabella*'s K. *lives, and will only live for her!*" O the comforting, the reviving impreffion! O the powerful medicine! How wonderfully has it recovered my almoft extinguifhed faculties! It is, Madam, to the power of that balm, that I have been enabled to move this far; and in confequence of this little billet, ferved up to me in a bafket of fome fruit, I have fome faint hopes of meeting this evening the only object of my cares. Be not then, dear Madam, fufpicious of the virtue of *Ifabella*; her foul never once was fufceptible to a tainted fentiment! She was proceeding, when their ears were attracted by the fteps of fome body approaching. The eager *Ifabella*, entertaining no other idea than of her long abfent *Killibarren*, gave the fignal to her companion to withdraw; but how miferably was fhe alarmed, when, in place of the moft amiable,

ble, fhe beheld, to her, the moft deteftable
of mankind, that infamous enemy to virtue,
the abandoned *Calender*, muffled up under
the difguife of a riding-coat! She fcreamed
out with all the feeble vehemence fhe could
collect: at firft he endeavoured to foften
her by a profufion of amorous proteftations,
all which fhe treated with the moft indignant repugnance: he then told her, that
her perfon, fortune, fame, and even her
life, were now at his difpofal; fhe was his
property by the concurrent difpofition of
her parents; and fhe was at the King's
mercy, from a proof of her having been in
a fecret correfpondence with an enemy and
traitor to the ftate. Thefe laft expreffions
aroufed her fmothered antipathy; Thofe
(replied fhe fharply) are the moft unworthy
of all traitors, who dare inftigate their king
to the exercife of injuftice and oppreffion,
and to ruin, pillage, and ravifh the un-
offending! Know, Sir, it is in that light I
have viewed the execrable *Calender!* in fo
much, that if you was the only man on
earth, *Ifabella* could never meet you with
her love. The enraged *Calender* laid hold
of the trembling victim; told her, in coarfeft
language, that it now mattered not whether
fhe approved him or not; but fwore, before they parted, he would enjoy by force
what fhe had fo long denied to folicitation.

S

Think

Think how wildly I was in that moment
agitated, to behold innocence and beauty,
and that innocence and beauty which had
awakened in me all the filial respect and
gratitude which her warm attachment to
the noble instrument of my existence could
call forth, now expofed to the violation of
a flagitious ruffian! to the humane propenfity of protecting the innocent, and dif-
charging fo immenfe a debt due to the
friends of a worthy father; think, I fay,
when in the author of this violation, I faw
before my eyes the inhuman murderer of
that father, how the terror of the *one*, and
the rapacity of the *other*, affected me, then
in a fituation which reftrained my offering
relief without the imminent hazard of my
own life, which was, however, a very light
confideration, compared to the much
weightier one of expofing my only bene-
factor, *Angus*'s daughter, the deareft object of my foul, and all his family, to inevitable deftruction. To fpeak, would have
been to little purpofe; I had no weapon
near me that could reach the ravager; the
wall was of fuch a height, that I muft have
maimed myfelf by an attempt to defcend
it: the natural feeblenefs of *Ifabella* rendered her incapable of refiftance; in groans
of agony, fhe lay motionlefs and fpeechlefs
in the villain's power; and he, pitilefs to
her

her expreffive fighs, was proceeding, by
bafe indecencies, to perpetrate his horrid
purpofe, when I got upon the wall, intending, at all events, to jump down upon him;
part of the wall crumbled down, which
alarmed the guilty villain; he left his prey
for a moment, to look round him; I profited of the advantage which was prefented
me by the mouldering wall; and loofening
fome of the ftones, at length became mafter
of one fo large, that I juft could move it.
with this ftone in my grafp, I watched my
opportunity, and directing its fall, I had
the good luck to founder him to the ground.
I repeated the blow, by aiming twenty more
at his guilty head, till at laft his impious groanings, and difability to move himfelf, gave me hopes that *Ifabella* was in that
juncture refcued: in a little time, I had the
fatisfaction to difcover, that fhe raifed herfelf from the ground, and in fearful trembling fteps, endeavoured to fteal herfelf from
the frightful fcene: I then loofened and
tumbled over a good deal more of the wall,
fo as to give the whole the appearance of
accident, and immediately retired very
quietly to my apartments.

' The dead body of *Calender* was found
the next morning, almoft covered with rub-
bifh and ftones: his partifans conjecturing
that it muft have been fome body from our

garden,

garden; I was immediately suggested to the
King, represented as mischievous in my
nature, and an inherent enemy to the King's
adherents. *Macbeth*, in extreme concern
for the death of *Calender*, who was in reality
become his chief favourite, deputed two or
three of his nearest relations to visit the garden, and make a strict examination into the
circumstances. *Eugenia* had missed me
longer than usual that evening; she catched
the alarm, questioned me about it, and I
candidly related to her the fact. Whilst
the courtiers were inspecting the place, she
officiously threw herself in the way; and
when she heard the circumstances of the
accident, and fearing the fatal effect it
might have upon me, she affected a hearty
sorrow, and, in presence of the inspectors,
cast herself at her father's feet, imploring
his forgiveness, if any accident had happened; said she was by chance walking
there in the dusk of the evening, and her
ears being surprised with an uncommon noise
from without the wall, she attempted to
loosen a stone to raise her so high as to see
over it, when, to her wonder, a considerable part of the wall gave way, fell to the
other side, and frightened her out of her
wits. The simplicity of this self-accusation
had the intended effect, and the inquirers
departed, fully satisfied that the misfortune
of

of their friend was purely the confequence of chance. How foon they were gone, the Thane and his fair daughter being joined by me, I had the mortification to hear her chid for being fo inattentive to what fhe was about, which the Thane aggravated, by the diftrefs he faid fhe might have innocently involved me into, as the only perfon fufpectable in his family. I was on the point of diverting his admonitions from the undeferving to the real object of them, which *Eugenia* perceiving, fuddenly prevented me, by offering her hand, and telling me, that our drawing-mafter had waited long for us.——Let the felfifh vanity of mankind, which arrogates to itfelf, 'in prejudice of the gentler, though more faithful fex, all the capacity for heroifm, blufh when they hear of this unexampled inftance of the nobleft friendfhip! You will not then wonder, my dear friends, who can relifh the force of fuch tranfcendent generofity, that I refpect and admire my *Eugenia* as the moft perfect model of both beauty and fentiment. I am forry that want of intelligence obliges me fo abruptly to leave the lamentable *Ifabella*: all our inquiries have never fince been able to trace her any farther than that night of danger; fhe fled from the feverities of her parents, but where, or how, it muft be left to time to

inform

inform us. I wifh fhe may not have proved to be one of many dreadful facrifices to the unreafonable rigour of unfeeling parents, who falfely judging, that the greateft human happinefs is only to be purchafed by fortune or grandeur, often precipitate their more fufceptible offspring to grafp even at the fhadows of felicity, in order to efcape parental aufterity; for if paternal admonitions and filial duties prove ineffectual, ı rftriction and feverity will, in place of prevailing, but aggravate the rifing defires. When growing paffions are checked by rigorous reftraint, they court every opportunity, howfoever perilous, to gratify the fmothered inclination; the interviews of the parties muft of neceffity be more private and retired; the more exquifite the temptation, the more unguarded the believing hearts of the moft innocent lovers; and where the paffion happens not to be under the guidance of unabating honour on both fides, a too implicit confidence may often land in the ruin of the moft deferving virgin! a fate which is more to be dreaded by an affectionate parent, than the moft difmal confequences that can attend matrimony in extremeft indigence.——But to return; if you think of that affectionate fympathy, which had already grown fo naturally into a mutual approbation between the dear

Eugenia

Eugenia and me, you who can feel, will easily conceive what strong impressions such an unexampled instance of the noblest generosity made upon my astonished senses: add to this, that *Eugenia* now advancing to her fourteenth year, began to disclose, with the rare accomplishments of a most elevated understanding, the blossoms of a personal beauty, that promised every perfection to be hoped for in the human constitution. It was on this occasion, that pouring out my grateful sentiments over her acquiescing bosom, both of us, I believe, begun to feel other emotions than those which had hitherto been the pure result of reciprocal approbation and esteem: I avowed to her the new, the tender sensations by which I then was agitated; I desired her to help me, if she could, to the use of such emphatic words as might best express them: it is, said I; more than gratitude, more than friendship, it is more than esteem, more than approbation, even more than admiration, and yet it is something that comprehends them all! O my incomparable *Eugenia!* it must be what we have sometimes read of; it must be what has been planted in my soul by Heaven, unknown to me; it must be love! I am never pleased but when you are with me; I am ever uneasy when you are out of my sight; my highest delight is in the

the charms of your voice; to touch you is
a fort of enchantment! Was ever fuch felicity before found in confinement? If this
is captivity, let me never be free, if that
freedom muft feparate me from *Eugenia*!

‘ The unufual expreffive blufhes which
now adorned the natural beauties of *Eugenia*, gave her, in fpite of every poffible
delicacy, the moft penetrating countenance.
Abafhed, and yet free from fhame, fhe modeftly replied, I have never, my dear *Lorn*,
difguifed my fentiments from you; nor will
I now; that efteem, that friendfhip, with
which I have ever regarded you, I find, as
well as you, have grown to a height, that
our beft readings but ill defcribe: it is impoffible, continued fhe, that my company
can be more pleafing to you, than yours is,
delightful to me; if it is love, let it be fo;
although I blufh, it fhould be no reproach
to own it; it was planted in the foil of innocence, and reared up in the funfhine of
virtue. In fuch endearing converfations
did the lovely *Eugenia* and I pafs the early
years of irreprehenfible communion. The
Thane and Lady *Angus* perceived our attachments, and happily it was not difguft-
ful to them. Her mother, upon her death-
bed, bequeathed her to my arms with un-
referved fatisfaction; and nothing retarded
the confummation of our felicity, but that
we

we durft not truft any mortal to give it the ceremonial fanction. At length, and but a fhort while before our flight, one honeft old clergyman, whofe years had then placed him beyond the obfervation of a guilty court, fought an afylum for his age, and was entertained by the Thane : he gave the hymeneal completion to our loves. Loving and beloved, we could then tafte of thofe joys, unknown to impurity, but chaftely longed for by thofe whofe paffions are limited by virtue. Love, prompted by luft, is ever indelicate ; prompted by ambition, it is feldom reciprocal ; and if conveniency is the only motive, it can never be ardent. But in mine and *Eugenia's*, delicacy, union and ardour, all concurred to confummate, with exquifite delight, our warmeft wifhes.

Lorn would have continued his narration, but was interrupted by a meffenger, who called upon *Edmund* to meet fome ftrangers who had juft alighted at his gate.

Edmund, after a fhort interval, returned, and with a remarkable fatisfaction in his countenance, introduced two gentlemen, one of whom was very quickly recognized by the *Scotch* Thanes to be an intimate companion and kinfman to the Thane of *Fife*. *Glamis* cordially faluted him ; *Angus* was advancing for the fame purpofe, when

Hamton

Hamton (*a*) (fo the gentleman was named) ftarted back with the wildeft look of con-fternation, aftonifhed to behold the man who, he ftill fuppofed, was minifter, and an abettor of *Macbeth*, in the fociety of thofe whofe aid he had come to follicit for that tyrant's extirpation. However, the myftery was foon unravelled, and gained entire credit by a brief explanation from *Glamis*. Young *Lorn* was made known, and a ge-neral harmony was confpicuous on every face. *Edmund* held in his hand a mandate from King *Edward*, forbidding all his faith-ful fubjects on the coafts and borders of *England*, to hold any fort of correfpondence with *Macbeth*, the pretended King of *Scot-land*, nor with any of his adherents or a-bettors; but to aid and fupport, to the ut-moft of their powers, *Malcolm*, the un-doubted and lawful heir to the crown of that kingdom. As the purport of this mandate filled every heart with unfpeak-able joy, they were impatient to know by what happy means it had been fo fuccefs-fully obtained; *Hamton*, with pleafure, pro-ceeded thus to fatisfy them.

(*a*) Afterwards *Hamilton*.

' When

" When the noble Thane of *Macduff*, faid he, took the refolution of flying from *Scotland*, his breaft was full of the glorious purpofe: he knew that *Malcolm*, whom he had always confidered as his King fince the murder of his father, was grandfon to *Sibert* Duke of *Northumberland*, a nobleman of the firft quality, and of great family con-nections in *England:* he learned alfo, that no nobleman at that court had more intereft, or was held in higher confideration with the renowned Earl *Godwin*, who was then a chief in the adminiftration of *Englifh* policy. On his arrival in *England*, he underftood, after fome inquiry, that *Malcolm* was then at court; thither he directed his journey as faft as poffible. The variety of devices that had been attempted to inveigle *Malcolm* down to *Scotland* by emiffaries from *Macbeth*, had made him very fhy and difficult of accefs to the natives of that kingdom; however, *Macduff* had himfelf introduced; and after the ftrongeft affurances of his loyal allegiance, he endeavoured to aroufe the dormant refentment of *Malcolm* againft the murderer of his father, and the difhonour of his country; he expatiated upon the prefent unpopularity and deteftable cha-racter of the Tyrant; bid him remember, that as he was the offspring of royal pro-genitors, he ought to fummon up an active, **princely**

princely fpirit, and endeavour, not only for
his own fake, but for the fake of a groaning
people, who would confider themfelves as
committed to his charge by the King of
Kings, to recover his paternal dignity, and
thereby carry relief to an oppreffed and
fpoiled nation. *Macduff* concluded, by telling him, that he confidered himfelf as the
reprefentative of every mortal in *Scotland*,
in whofe breafts there remained the fmalleft
fparks of honour or of virtue; that it was
in their names, not in his own only, that
he had hazarded all that was precious to
him, to difcover the true ftate of things to
his King, with whom he was ready to fhare
in the worft, or the beft difpenfations of
fortune.

' *Malcolm*, uncommonly cautious for his
years, liftened with greedy attention, but
replied with fufpicion : he was defirous to
make a very fure trial of *Macduff*'s fincerity; and therefore, fuppreffing thofe emotions which he really felt, " I am not infenfible (faid he) to the oppreffions under
which my country bleeds; nor do I imagine that the tyrannies imputed to the
Ufurper are by any means exaggerated;
and the inducements for a Prince to enterprize a reformation in fuch a cafe, are
doubtlefs very urging : but I am afraid,
my good Thane, your inftances would not
be

be fo prefling with me to affume the regal
authority, if you was better acquainted
with my native difpofitions. Let me not
deceive you then, but fairly confefs, that
the fame vices which have already been the
ruin of many kings, luft and avarice, are
too predominant in me, not to defeat the
very purpofes you expect from me. It is
true, that my want of power, and the private condition I have lived in, have fo
greatly reftrained the exertion of them,
that the world think more favourably of
me than I deferve; but was I to be cloathed
with kingly power and uncontroulable authority, the reins which at prefent are a
check upon thefe vices, would be loofened,
and my hearkening to your importunities
on this head, might more probably involve
us in greater miferies, than reftore to you
and the country that tranquillity you hope
for." *Macduff* wondered; but calmly obferved, That the firft ftep towards reformation, was to have a fenfe of thofe errors
which were apt to mifguide us; that a
rambling defire for women was natural to
the moft of young men, but was often conquered by the more folid and agreeable pleafures that were to be found in the arms of
a well chofen companion for life; that the
more unmanly luft of avarice had been often
propagated by the apprehenfions of want,

the

the fear of which would be totally banished
from the breast of *Malcolm*, so soon as he
should accomplish the possession of his father's dominions; and finally said, that
that avarice must indeed be extremely in-
satiable, which is not to be satisfied with
the revenues of a kingdom. *Malcolm* persisted in objecting; and concluded by telling him, that there were still other weak-
nesses, and yet more unbecoming a king,
which he knew himself liable to, and which
would make him and the nation sadly re-
pent of their choice, should he acquiesce in
their loyal invitation: There is (says he)
no truth nor sincerity in me! Undeserving
of confidence myself, I can put confidence
in no man! I am by nature changeable,
incapable of forming friendships; and so
unreasonably suspicious, that those who
should be the most forward in my service,
might be the first who should feel the sad
effects of my jealous temper; for from the
inconstancy of my own nature, I judge of
the dispositions of all other men. At this
moment (continued he) my jealousy moves
me to the strongest suspicions against the
honesty of *Macduff*.

‘ *Macduff*, unable to confine any longer
his swelling indignation, exclaimed, from
heart-felt distress; Avaunt then, thou disgrace to royalty! thou dishonour to thy
family!

family! O my country! O my bleeding country! Are all hopes of thy redemption thus paſt away? It muſt not be; that crown which the daſtard ſon of *Duncan* confeſſes himſelf unworthy to wear, may well be an additional ornament to the brow of the more meritorious *Edward!* I go about it; he ſhall be invited to conquer, and to enjoy it. *Macduff* appeared ready to abandon him; but *Malcolm*, fully ſatisfied of the Thane's ſincerity, caught hold of him; Stay, my dear Thane, ſaid he, ſtay, thou pattern of loyal patriotiſm; forgive the trial I have made of thy fidelity, which thou haſt ſo well proved by that indignant paſſion which the ſuppoſed frailties, even of the man you deſire to make your ſovereign, has inſpired you with! How different yours from the ſycophantiſh behaviour of thoſe emiſſaries employed to ſeduce me by *Macbeth?* the more villainous I could repreſent myſelf to them, the more they courted me, the more they counted me fit for the vile purpoſes of a proſtituted government: it was therefore, my dear *Macduff*, that I was afraid of every temptation that was preſented to me to regain my country; it was therefore that I arraigned myſelf as a wretch under the dominion of ſuch vicious principles, as my honeſt ſoul ſhuddered within me at the bare mention of! But I am convinced, it is not

the

the greatneſs of your fortune, the grandeur of your family, nor the reputation of your honour, that has thus convinced me; it is a nobleneſs, a ſanctity of manners, better expreſſed through your looks than from your tongue, that diſpoſes me now to embrace you with all the confidence of a truſty friend. Be then my *Mentor*, lead me on to the arduous, the glorious taſk, of getting juſtice for my ſuffering country, my injured family, and oppreſſed people!——If the ſoul of *Macduff* was at firſt tortured with the odious picture which *Malcolm* had preſented of himſelf, what joy did he now feel in beholding the reverſe? He fell down before him! hailed him King! and drawing his ſword, vowed never more to ſheath it, until he ſhould ſee the ſovereignty, credit, and tranquillity of his country, reſtored. Thus the ſtricteſt and moſt cordial engagements being mutually concluded, it was immediately reſolved, by the intereſt of *Malcolm's* grandfather and the Earl *Godwin*, to ſupplicate aſſiſtance from King *Edward*, who, by the way, had hitherto been deaf to every ſuggeſtion of that ſort; for amidſt all the diſſipation which ſo much ſcandalized the court of *Macbeth*, he had ſtill had policy enough, by maintaining a ſubmiſſive correſpondence with the court of *England*, to keep up ſuch an alliance with *Edward*, as to

to fcreen himfelf from fo dangerous a refentment : and at this very juncture he kept
one of the moft politic of his creatures,
whom he had dignified with the title of
Thane of *Monteith*, as his reprefentative in
England for that purpofe. *Monteith*, who
was extremely artful, was a conftant fpy
upon every motion of *Malcolm*'s ; and having traced him in his moft fecret interviews
with *Macduff* ; and eafily guefling at their
purpofe, took care to get *Macduff* reprefented to the court of *England* in fuch a
difadvantageous light, as to weaken his
applications. But in the height of thefe
difficulties, I happened to arrive, and
brought to *Macduff* the firft account of the
woeful barbarities which had been perpetrated in his family. With what heart-
rending horrors did he hear the fhocking
tale ! He flew to *Malcolm*, whofe generous
heart was no lefs penetrated with the fad
relation than his own. *Malcolm* taking
Macduff and myfelf alongft with him, went
immediately to court, demanded and obtained an audience of *Edward*; before whom
I was examined ; and producing other well
authenticated vouchers of every circumftance of the fatal cataftrophe, fo effectually
awakened fympathy and refentment in the
foul of good King *Edward*, that he inftantly
refolved, maugre all other confiderations,

to

to support *Malcolm* through the difficult operations he had undertaken; and, as the first proof of his being in earnest, he issued immediate orders to forbid *Monteith*, or any other on the part of *Macbeth*, to enter the court of England; and further ordered, that *Monteith* should retire from *England* within three days. Nothing now remaining to obstruct our solicitations at the court of *Edward*, five thousand chosen men were mustered, and put under the command of the Duke of *Northumberland*, who, accompanied by *Malcolm*, are actually on their march hither, that they may be joined by an equal number of borderers; and as soon as completed, they have orders to proceed directly for *Scotland*: upon entering that kingdom, *Malcolm* is to be proclaimed King, to set up the *Scotch* standard, and then to have the command of the whole, as well *English* as *Scotch*. It would be torturing language to search for words to express the joy that now appeared in every face, when Mr. *Hamton* had finished his interesting relation; and a few days more added to it a very affecting circumstance. It should have been sooner observed, that the generous *Edmund*, impatient to consummate the felicity of his admired guests, had freighted a small vessel, and dispatched her to *Ila*, there to make inquiry after the
venerable

venerable Thane of *Argyle*. This veffel now returned, and bleffed the expecting company with the prefence of that noble Thane, attended by the brave and faithful *Killibarren*, a name the reader is not a ftranger to. Fain would the author attempt a defcription of thofe different and lively fenfations which at this joyful conjuncture muft have been communicated from one to another of this tranfported affembly; but it would be in vain! Think, fenfible reader, of the virtuous *Lorn*, furprifed with the appearance of a moft refpectable parent, whom, from his earlieft years, even until now, he had been taught to lament as dead! Think, I fay, what muft be thofe filial feelings which then enchanted him; and add to it, that paternal fondnefs diftinguifhed in every feature of a father, who had already counted fo lightly of hazarding his fortune and his life for the prefervation of a darling fon! You muft fuppofe it all: the moft powerful efforts of poetry or painting would but ill defcribe them. Suffice it then to fay, that fuch another difplay of contentment and reciprocal happinefs was never perhaps fo eminent in one and the fame fociety.

Edmund was fo entirely tranfported with the joyous profpect of feeing thefe worthy noblemen regain their native liberty

berty and poffeffions, that he forgot himfelf as in retirement : he got his equipages ready ; and propofing to accompany his friends in their expedition, he was extremely active in levying troops to join them. A few days only paffed, when they received a courier from *Malcolm*, to let them know, that the Duke of *Northumberland*, with the van of the *Englifh* army, was advanced as far as *Halifax* in *Yorkfhire*, and was proceeding to *Lancafter*, where he would halt two days, to wait the junction of their friends in thefe parts ; thence pafs through *Cumberland*, make another halt at *Carlifle* for three days, and then enter *Scotland* with all poffible expedition. Upon this intelligence, the generous *Edmund*, the Thanes of *Argyle* and *Glamis*, *Lorn*, *Killibarren*, and Mr. *Hamton*, were all accoutred, and ready, at the head of about 400 men, to march to join their friends at *Lancafter*. The Thane of *Angus*, notwithftanding all entreaties, and that every one of the company was now become as fincerely his friend, as they had formerly been the reverfe, would by no means be prevailed with to undertake a fhare in the enterprize. He faid, that although their condefcendance for him had induced them to excufe his adminiftration in *Scotland*, that the people in general of that country would not

fee

fee with fo favourable eyes; and that as diffidence was a faculty more natural to mankind than approbation, he was afraid, that his appearing with the army in the character his birth intitled him to, might rather hurt than forward his Sovereign's caufe; befides, he faid, he could not totally exculpate himfelf, for that too flavifh fubmiffion with which he had fo long bended to the will of tyranny; that his upright intentions, and the few laudable actions for which their goodnefs had juftified the whole purport of his conduct, did not amount to a fufficient abfolution in his own mind: that it was his refolution never more to return to *Scotland*, but to linger out the reft of his exiftence in penitence, with the good real Hermit who had affifted in faving his life. Every body endeavoured to diffuade him from this refolution, but in vain: *Argyle*, and *Lorn*, his fon-in-law, importuned him in the moft moving language; he was determined; and concluded by telling his noble friend *Argyle*, that as for many years paft, the only circumftance which made life worthy of his care, was the concern which paternal love infpired him with for the prefervation and happinefs of *Lorn* and his darling daughter; and as that was now devolved upon another, much more able and refpectable parent, he would retire from the
world

world with pleafure, fettle his accounts with Heaven, and pray unwearied for their fuccefs and profperity. It was even with difficulty, that the pious tears of his daughter, enforced with the perfuafive eloquence of the amiable *Bertha*, could prevail with him to poftpone his felf-feclufion, that he might by his company mitigate a little of that tirefomenefs which they were willingly to fuffer during the abfence of their Lords. To their folicitations, however, at length he yielded; and every thing being now as much fettled at the houfe of *Edmund*, as, under fuch interefting circumftances, could poffibly be, a very affecting farewell feparated the different parties.

In a few days our patriots arrived at *Lancafter*, and with their fquadron joined the main body. Never was there a more cordial meeting than now felicitated the hopeful Chieftans : *Malcolm*, with joy unutterable, welcomed his venerable friends, the Thanes of *Argyle* and *Glamis*; and *Macduff*, unable to confine his tranfport, interrupted even the greetings of his King : ' Thrice-welcome (cried he) my noble fellow fufferers ! Let me congratulate you and myfelf on the eminent profpect now prefented to us of chaftifing a long exerted tyranny and oppreffion over a groaning country ! What unexampled excitements have we to
lead

lead us on to the glorious enterprize! But it is ufelefs to wafte time to inftigate you ; you feel as warmly as I do ; but you muft forgive the overflowings of a friend's heart, who by one effort of the Tyrant's barbarity, was beggared! difhonoured! widowed! and rendered childlefs ! Yours and our country's wrongs may, and, by the help of God, they will be redreffed ; but mine, alas! never can ; O my wife! O my children !" The fenfible heart of *Edmund* was ready to burft, on perceiving the manly anguifh which thus overcame the gallant *Macduff* ; when *Glamis*, by a feafonable interruption of the growing diftrefs, gave a turn to the woeful fubject, by recommending to *Macduff*'s attention the illuftrious *Edmund*, and relating fome of his exalted virtues.

The Duke of *Northumberland* had taken the advantage of the halt to pafs through *Weftmoreland*, and thence into his own country, to give the neceffary orders in thofe parts ; and propofed only to rejoin the army at *Carlifle* ; for which place they next day continued their march, under the command of *Malcolm:* and now coufiderable reinforcements from the *Scotch* fide were adding every hour to their ftrength, when the van arrived at *Carlifle*. The Duke entered it the fame day at the head of 1500 *Northumbrians*

brians and *Cumberland*-men : the Duke of *Northumberland* quickly recognized his kinfman *Edmund*, and was overjoyed to fee him once more in a fcene of action ; nor was he lefs happy on being made acquainted with the renowned Thanes of *Argyle* and *Glamis*, and the Lord of *Lorn*, the patriotic fame of each of whom had reached and often charmed his ears. It was then they held the firft council of war. They received intelligence from the *Scots* who had joined them, many of whom had embraced the firft opportunity of flying from under the command of tyranny, that *Macbeth* having heard of the march of the *Englifh*, and fearing a revolt of the Southern *Scots*, had actually advanced, with fuch an army as he could mufter, as far as the *Tiviot* hills, and had formed feveral flying encampments, intending thereby not only to interrupt the revolting *Scots* from joining with the *Englifh*, but to offer the *Englifh* battle from fome advantageous poft among the hills ; but that having heard of the numbers of the *Englifh* army, which had been greatly magnified, and that the Thanes of *Argyle* and *Glamis* (both of whom he counted dead) as well as *Macduff*, were with them, he was ftruck with horror and difmay, and immediately meditated a retreat ; judging, if he fhould be compelled to give battle at

laft,

last, he should fight with more advantage in the North, be more in the centre of his adherents, and be better able to fatigue and harrass the *English* troops, by marches thro' hills and mountains they were not accustomed with.

Mean while the confederate army (for so they may now be stiled) moved into *Scotland* without the smallest interruption. The standard of *Malcolm* was set up at *Annand*; he was proclaimed King of *Scotland* amidst resounding acclamations of applause, and took upon him the command of the whole army : he confirmed in *Sibert*, his grandfather, the chief command of the *English*, and appointed his illustrious friend *Edmund* a lieutenant-general; and the same rank for *Scotland* was bestowed upon *Argyle*, *Glamis*, and *Macduff*. They continued marching, and accumulating numbers every hour. The *English* troops were astonished, when at this time they found themselves in the heart of a country, where they imagined they were to meet their enemies, not to see nor hear of any but friends, and the most joyful salutations of a hearty welcome: they therefore proceeded in such spirits, as must have subdued *Macbeth*, if he could have assembled an army equal to *Malcolm*'s.

Macbeth perceiving that his army hourly diminished, at length, unwilling at any rate

U

to

to hazard a battle, betook himself for safety to his castle of *Dunsinane*, and formed a scattered sort of encampment around it, composed of those adherents, who having so long associated with him in every sort of criminality, knew that their only chance to escape such a fate as was the due to unremitting villanies, was to risk their lives alongst with their leader.

The royal party continued their advances to *Dunsinane*; and at *Bernham* wood, as a token that they hoped to accomplish a conquest without slaughter, the troops, by order of *Malcolm*, plumed their hats with oaken boughs; and then making a motion for surrounding the castle, *Macbeth*, who had taken a view of them from a turret, was hopeless and confounded! he regarded their strength, numbers, and regularity, as irresistible! Consciousness now penetrated his guilty soul; he was desperate and distracted; he threatened his own, and the life of every person who came near him: his wife, who had been at all times ready to assist in his schemes of cruelty, was more obnoxious to him than a haggard witch; he reproached her with the most pungent upbraidings; she recriminated with equal fury and desperation; and they were often on the point of hurrying each other into that eternity, which of all things they

dreaded

dreaded the moſt, but which would not
have been deferred a ſingle moment by any
thing leſs than the terrible picture which
their cankered conſciences had formed of it.
They flew, deſpondent, from the hateful
ſight of one another; and in fine, he, and
the whole of his party, being overwhelmed
in the ſame marks of deſpair, became the
moſt hideous objects of one another. *Dun-
ſinane* now was hell in epitome! every moving figure bore the reſemblance of a devil!
At length the enemy being juſt ready, with
ſword in hand, to force the gates, *Macbeth*
diſguiſed himſelf in the habit of a common
trooper, and leaving his friends at the mercy
of the conquerors, and anxious, as a condemned malefactor, to poſtpone the awful
plunge, ſought his eſcape through a private
poſtern. By this time the royal troops had
entered the caſtle: *Macduff*, from whoſe
breaſt the ideas of ſpoiled honour, the un-
pitied ſighs of a raviſhed and murdered
wife, and the unmoving cries of maſſacred
children, could never be baniſhed, was the
firſt that forced his way; he ran, fearleſs,
to and fro, in ſearch of the ſpoiler; at length
one of the banditti, hoping to recommend
himſelf to mercy, pointed out the little back
gate through which the monſter had fled;
Macduff purſued, and found him, with a
few of his partiſans, attempting to ſcramble

over

over a wall, the corner of a baſtion : the noiſe of *Macduff*'s ſhouting alarmed the delinquents, whoſe eſcape being now impracticable, a falſe bravery grew upon their deſpair : *Macbeth* turned, with all the briſkneſs he could ſummon, to defend himſelf ; and *Macduff*, who, maugre his diſguiſe, inſtantly knew him, ſingled him out for his immediate vengeance : the Tyrant fought with ſkill ; but guiltineſs enfeebling his nerves, he was unequal to the ſuperior force of *Macduff*'s unerring arm, which, after a few ſlighter paſſes, by one furious and well aimed blow, brought him, reeling, in mutterings unſanctified, to the ground ! The vengeful *Macduff* repeated his blows, and could not reſtrain himſelf from puſhing home every wound with exprobations on the maſſacre of his family.

Thus fell the wretch who had got himſelf exalted to dignities by virtues to which he had been ſchooled, but which not being natural to him, he could not perſevere in ; and had diſgraced the character of a Prince by the exerciſe of vices which had been born with him, but which he had the guile to ſmother whilſt in the rank of a private perſon.

The ſhame of womankind, the inſtigator, as well as partner of all his flagitiouſneſs, his wife, was found dead next day in the outſide of the caſtle ; ſhe having, in the

transport

transport of despondency, flung herself over the wall of one of the ramparts. *Malcolm* ordered both their bodies to be decently buried, in respect to the families they had the honour to be sprung from ; but their heads, that the memory of their wickedness might serve as an antidote to posterity, were exhibited to public view upon two spears erected on the top of a high tower ; and between them there was raised the figure of a serpent with a double head, each head inclining to those of the victims, as if hissing, and equally directing its baneful influence at both of them. His adherents, excepting such as, through their resistance, were slain, were all made prisoners. A court extraordinary was ordained to try them, when *Malcolm* was graciously pleased to remit the crime of rebellion, and to declare those only condemnable to suffer death, against whom there were separate proofs of murders, rapes, or other violent depredations ; an example of justice tempered with a clemency worthy the imitation of more enlightened ages.

Never was so sudden a revolution accomplished with so little bloodshed, nor was there ever a restoration of right with more universal applause. The unanimity which governed the *English* and *Scottish* Chiefs, prevented the least tendency to

jealoufies; and the *Englifh* troops returned
to their own kindom with the fatisfaction of
having been inftrumental, without the lofs
of a man, of re-eftablifhing their neighbouring nation in a ftate of tranquillity unknown to them for many years; leaving
behind them, as well as carrying with them,
an early proof of the great utility of a cordial union between fo near neighbours,
when combined in the great caufe of liberty
and juftice.

A day was named for the coronation
of *Malcolm* at *Scoon*; and at his earneft in-
treaties, his grandfather and the noble *Edmund* were prevailed upon to be witneffes
of the folemnity. The day appointed came,
and immediately after *Malcolm* had taken
the coronation oath, the venerable Thane
of *Argyle* delivered himfelf to this effect:

' I truft in God, my Sovereign Liege,
' that the virtues of your own conftitution,
' more than the dreadful example of your
' wicked predeceffor, will guide you a-
' gainft all the errors of the paft reign:
' with the regal dignity, you are invefted
' with the difpofal of places of profit, of
' power and of honour: be thefe beftowed
' without partiality; let the weight of me-
' rit, not the chance of birth, be intitled
' to preference in the purchafe. Society
' was inftituted by heaven, and a defire for
' it

it impelled in the mind from the creation of the world; without it, exiftence would have been a burden; The good of that fociety, we may believe, was the great aim of the Omnipotent Being who formed. it: You are his vicegerent; and the happinefs of your *people* ought to be your firft, your chief and conftant ftudy, if you hope to acquit yourfelf as an honeft man before that King, who had the power to make you *theirs*, and by whofe indulgence alone you can expect to reign happily. You may now look upon yourfelf as the favourite of Heaven; fo for a while might *Macbeth!* and fo he might have continued, had he acted confiftently with the facred oaths he took, and which you have now taken: but he deviated from the paths of virtue; he gave a loofe to vicious paffions; he valued only fuch favourites as flattered his vices; he forfook the true interefts of his people, and the King of Kings forfook him. Of all other mifchiefs, beware of *favourites!* A Governor fhould have no ftate favourites, but fuch whofe conduct has rendered them worthy the confidence of the governed; the laws will then exert their vigour without obftruction; there will be no murmurings; criminals will calmly fubmit to punifhments, becaufe they are
' inflicted

' inflicted by laws of their own approving?
' To fay that a King is to have no perfonal
' favourites, would be to fay, that the King
' muſt be more than human ; it is abfurd ;
' whilſt a King is mortal, he will be under
' the influence of mortal paſſions ; but let
' him be careful to diſtinguiſh between the
' *favourite* of his private amuſements, and
' the *favourite* of public adminiſtrations .
' the difference may be likened unto that
' of a gentleman's family ; a very fenfible
' worthy man may be infpired with affec-
' tions for different companions, who may
' lighten his cares, divert his leifure hours,
' and be in many refpects moſt agreeable
' to him ; yet, perhaps, amongſt all thefe
' his moſt approved friends, he may not
' find one properly qualified to be a pre-
' ceptor for his children. Such a depart-
' ment requires talents peculiar to itſelf ;
' it requires an application to the various
' tempers to be dealt with, which very few
' of thefe moſt eſteemed friends, if they
' have the underſtanding, have alfo the pa-
' tience to beſtow upon them. So it is,
' my Liege, in the family political, the
' ſtate : you will difcover in many of your
' nobles different qualities, that may ren-
' der them perfonally amiable to you ; but
' he is a prodigy of a man, who poſſeſſes
' every qualification neceſſary to an admi-
                            ' niſtrator.

' niftrator. There are none of us totally
' free from vanity; and how foon we can
' gain a King's favour for us in one point,
' we flatter our own abilities, we fuppofe
' we are omnifcious, and then labour to
' worm ourfelves fo entirely into power,
' that it is too late for our mafter to look
' at things through his own eyes, he muft
' look through ours. Others, who do not
' confider us with the fame prejudices, are
' more inquifitive into our foibles : when
' we have arrived at the fummit of our am-
' bition, we are lefs anxious to pleafe, we
' are lefs upon our guard, and our weak-
' neffes are difcovered ; thefe weakneffes
' are imputed to the King ; and thus, on
' account of a defigning *favourite*, has the
' beft of kings become often the derifion,
' fometimes the deteftation, of his fubjects.
' Be then cautious, my Liege, let me again
' repeat it, be cautious in the choice of
' your minifters; if you have a perfonal
' favourite, honour him with your efteem
' for thofe good difpofitions which have re-
' commended him ; but unlefs he has the
' concurring voice of your fubjects, let him
' be the laft man you would pitch upon for
' your minifter, left the prejudices pre-
' conceived in his favour fhould make you
' blind to errors which will be perceived
' by your people, who by reafon of your
                              ' preference,

' preference, will be the more fuspicious;
' and, next to God, it is to his people to
' whom a king is accountable. But should
' a *popular minifler* deviate (which may
' often happen) from their expectations,
' the confequence will be, that in place of
' imputing his errors to the Sovereign, it
' will have the reverfe effect; they will
' blame their own choice, and with a more
' implicit confidence, throw themfelves en-
' tirely upon Majefty for redrefs. When
' a fubject, through prejudice, partiality,
' or paffion, injures his neighbour, he is
' liable to the laws for the offence he has
' done againft fociety : if a private perfon
' then has a legal remedy for wrongs fuf-
' tained from the paffions of his neighbour,
' has not the Public as juft a title to redrefs
' for injuries fuftained through the preju-
' dices of their Prince ? certainly; and the
' more fo, in fo far as *public* is preferable
' to *individual* intereft.

' I dwell the longer upon this fubject,
' my Liege, that it was *favouritifm* that
' proved a bane to the reign of your royal
' father; he was continually embarraffed
' between two favourites, the Thanes of
' *Rofs* and *Caithnefs*; each had his faction;
' and as the King was unwilling to difoblige
' either of them, they rofe and fell alter-
' nately; they had no other views than to
' enrich

enrich and aggrandize their respective
parties; the national interest was quite
neglected; the people grew discontented,
they sought a change, and they have been
punished by what they courted. You,
my Liege, mount the throne of your father with every earthly advantage; you
are seated in the love of your people;
you are happy in the approbation of your
nobles: Let the voice of the *public* find,
on all occasions, free access to your councils; and be ever suspicious of that favourite who shall endeavour to suppress
their complaints, or poison your ears with
the baneful sound of *prerogative* and *ab-
solute power*. A favourite will, for the most
part, have some interested projects to promote: from the Public voice you may
sometimes hear mistaken, but rarely dis-
honest counsel: the people have no interest to deceive you, because, by deceiv-
ing you, they deceive themselves. Begin
your reign by enquiring into, and re-
dressing their grievances; when they are
mistaken, correct them, but with a fa-
therly hand, to the end that they may not
fear without esteeming you. Proceed,
with the assistance of your nobles and
able counsellors, to collect and form
from the records a system of wholesome
laws; introductive to which, permit me,

' my

' my Sovereign Liege, to prefent you with
' a *gift*, preferved from the ravaging hands
' of ufurpation, which, although two hun-
' dred years old, yet which, if obferved and
' wifely improved, will be a diadem no lefs
' ornamental to a royal heart, than a crown
' to the royal head : here, my Lige, *(pre-*
' *fenting a fcroll of parchment) (a)* is an
' authenticated duplicate of the *falutary*
' *laws* inftituted by your illuftrious prede-
' ceffor, *Kennethus* II. when after the ex-
' tirpation of the faithlefs *Picts,* your an-
' cient kingdom was enlarged, and firft got
' the name of *Scotland.* Let thefe laws be
' revifed ; and wherein any change of cir-
' cumftances has rendered it neceffary, let
' them be altered or amended : let them
' next be proclaimed for the public fanc-
' tion ; and having once got *that,* abide
' and govern by them. Nothing fo con-
' temptibly betrays the feeblenefs of go-
' vernment, than this day to pronounce an
' edict that may pleafe one faction, and to
' abolifh it the next, to humour another :
' by fuch a conduct your laws will multiply ;
' multiplicity of laws will generate chi-
' canery ; chicanery will create expence ;
' rich villainy will triumph over indigent

(a) See a Copy of thefe Laws in the Conclufion,
at Pages 234, &c.

' honefty ;

honesty; and the poor will feelingly com-
plain of oppression. The affiance between
a king and his subjects ought to be held
as the most sacred compact; it is plain of
itself; it requires but few laws to establish
and to maintain it; and it should never
be perplexed with knotty arguments.
Like a contract between husband and
wife, let the laws you assent to, and your
coronation oath, be an inviolable contract
between you and your people; then, my
Liege, they will find it their supreme
happiness to love and obey their Sovereign, as you, I hope, will find it yours,
to cherish, support, and improve the
rights of the Public. That it may be so,
and that with a reign just, happy, and
glorious, you may enjoy long life with
health and satisfaction, is, and while I
have breath to draw, shall be my most
fervent prayer.'

This truly noble and patriotic harangue
met with the approbation it deserved. The
King descended from the coronation chair,
embraced *Argyle*, and thanked him for his
loyal and affectionate advice, with such an
air of candid affability, as demonstrated
that it had been sincerely agreeable to
him.

X   The

The firſt act of his ſovereign will was to create the Thane, Earl of *Argyle*, a title till then not known in *Scotland*: then turning immediately to the other nobles, (each of whom were ſoon diſtinguiſhed by titles adequate to their reputation and families) he told them, " That he would begin his reign, at leaſt, by a deference to that advice which he had with ſo much pleaſure attended to, in conferring a new and honourable title upon the man who had had the honeſty to read him ſo proper a leſſon ; and he hoped that he ſhould thereby convince his ſubjects, that the moſt direct road to his favour ſhould be at all times to approach him with *truth*."

The

The LAWS and STATUTES ordained by King *Kennethus*, were as followeth.

I. ANY perſon that blaſphemeth, or diſreſpecteth God or his ſaints, ſhall, in the firſt place, be deprived of the tongue ; and any who ſhall abuſe the King or Chief Captain, may be puniſhed in the ſame manner.

II. All men convicted of murder, ſhall be hanged, or loſe the head ; and if convicted of theft, they ſhall be hanged. Any woman convicted of a capital crime, ſhall be drowned or buried alive.

III. Any one making lies, to the damage of his neighbour, ſhall loſe his ſword, and be baniſhed from good company.

IV. He that raviſheth a virgin, (unleſs ſhe marry him) ſhall be beheaded.

V. He that defileth another man's wife, ſhall be put to death with the woman, unleſs the woman be forced.

VI. He that forceth any woman, and the violence made evident, ſhall be beheaded, and the woman declared innocent.

X 2   VII. A wife

VII. A wife may not be punifhed for a hufband's crime; but a hufband fhall be punifhed for the crime of his wife, if he knew of it: if it be a concubine, fhe fhall be punifhed as the man.

VIII. All oppreffors, or invaders of other men's lands, fhall be beheaded.

IX. All vagabonds and idle perfons fhall be, in the firft place, marked with a burn on the cheek; and if they perfevere in idlenefs, they may be whipt, or even hanged.

X. If any fon injure his parents by word or deed, he fhall firft lofe either tongue, hand, or foot, whereby he offended the parent, and then be hanged, and his body remain unburied.

XI. If a parent contradicts nature, and caufelefsly is cruel to his fon; the fon muft feek redrefs from the King, or the udge of the fhire.

XII. Any fon who may be difloyal to the King, or to his parent, who has been, or may be born dumb, deaf, or foolifh, may be difinherited.

XIII. No

XIII. No fon, not even the King's fon, after the death of a father, fhall be deemed capable, before the age of 21, to take upon him the charge of his father's family ; but that charge may be tranfmitted by teftament to fome kinfman ; and in default of teftament on the King's part, the kinfman is to be chofen by the King's counfellors ; or if a fubject, the neareft of kin, he being *compos mentis.* The eldeft fon of the King, a noble, or honourable, is of right, and if habile, to inherit the power, lands and honours, of the father, as the father came to them, or even if he has added to them ; yet it may be in a father's power to divide what moveable goods or wealth he may in his own time have acquired, amongft his other offspring, according to their deferts : but if the father himfelf has made no fuch divifion, the offspring muft inherit equally. So it may be with others who have no children ; they may, by a laft will, bequeath their moveable riches to whom they pleafe ; but in default, the neareft of kin to inherit as an eldeft fon, who may neverthelefs be adjudged by the King or judge of the fhire to difpenfe with a reafonable proportion out of his eftate, to prevent others who are in the fame kinfhip, and cannot earn a livelihood, from being beggarly, or a difcredit to the family.

X 3   XIV. No

XIV. No man shall sow his corn till the weeds be taken from the good grain ; and he that defileth his land with weeds, shall pay for the first fault an ox, for the second, ten oxen, and forfeit the land, if he transgresseth a third time.

XV. If a beast be found going astray, it shall be by the finder given to the searchers for theft, or to the parish priest, to be kept for the owner ; if it be kept up three days, the person who kept it shall be held as a thief.

XVI. If any person taketh or detaineth any kind of goods or beasts belonging to his neighbour, and restoreth not after proclamation made, he shall be deemed and punished as a thief.

XVII. If any man's cattle eat his neighbour's corn, the cattle may be poinded, till the owner redress the skaith done by his cattle.

XVIII. Swine that eat their young shall be killed, and their flesh forbidden.

XIX. Churches, altars, sacred images, chapels, oratories, priests, and all ecclesiastic persons, shall be held in reverence.

He

He that hurts a churchman in word or deed, may be punished to death, unless the churchman forgive and intercede for him.

XX. Festivals, fasts, vigils, and other solemn ceremonies of the church, shall be observed according to the ecclesiastical constitution. Sepulchres shall also be held in reverence, and a cross put on them, that none may tread thereon.

XXI. The corpses of dead persons shall be buried with a funeral according to their circumstances : if a nobleman that has done great actions, two horsemen shall pass before him to the church ; the one arrayed in his best cloathing, bearing his armour and weapons on a white horse ; the other shall pass in a mournful posture, clad in black, on a horse of the same colour ; and when the corpse is entered the church, the man riding the black horse shall turn his back to the altar, and there lament and deplore the death of the defunct ; and when the corpse is entered, he shall return the same way that he came, but the other shall offer his white horse and armour to the priest.

XXII. If a man will seduce a maiden under the age of 20, that she thereby lose her good name, he shall maintain her, (and children,

children, if any) according to her parentage, till she be married. If any man is willing to marry her, the seducer must give her a dowry according to his circumstances ; and if a husband, who accepteth such wife and dowry, shall afterwards reproach her with it, he may be punished by the ordinary judge.

XXIII. To preserve order, every person who comporteth not in a kindly fashion to his equals, and respectfully to his superiors, may be fined, imprisoned or whipped, according to the degree of his offence. So may Sabbath-breakers, gluttons and drunkards, if by Sabbath-breaking, drinking or gluttony, they injure or offend their neighbour.

XXIV. That the King ordain for every shire, a man well born, who has been taught to read and write, as a competent judge, who must always reside in the shire, to decide all controversies betwixt the subjects ; but in case of crimes punishable by death, the judge must call to his aid an inquest of seven, nine, eleven, thirteen, fifteen, or any other odd number of judicious men, of the same degree with the criminal, the major number of whom is to declare, Whether he is innocent or guilty ? If an ecclefiaftic fall from his comportment, and, upon an inqueft of clergy, fhall be declared to have tranf-greffed againft any of the King's ftatutes, his cloak muft be pulled off by a deacon, who muft deliver him over to the judge of the fhire, and he to deal with him as a layick.

XXV. If any difpute of right fhould fpring up between the King and a fub-ject, the fame muft be decided by the major part of the King's council : and if it fhould be made appear to the King, with his lawful council, that any one of the judges of fhires, or even any of the King's counfellors, have, from corruptible-nefs of heart, pronounced unfair judgment, and have not abided by the laws and in-ftitutions of the kingdom, as fettled by the facred oath of coronation, and written upon thefe records ; fuch counfellor or judge, being convicted, fhall, maugre the interceffion of ecclefiaftics, be hung by the neck, until he be dead, upon a high gibbet.

F I N I S.

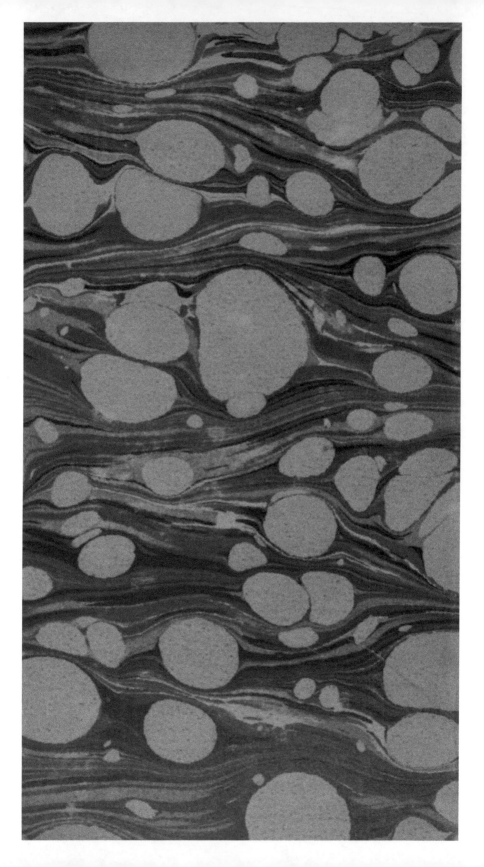

Check Out More Titles From HardPress Classics Series In this collection we are offering thousands of classic and hard to find books. This series spans a vast array of subjects – so you are bound to find something of interest to enjoy reading and learning about.

Subjects:
Architecture
Art
Biography & Autobiography
Body, Mind &Spirit
Children & Young Adult
Dramas
Education
Fiction
History
Language Arts & Disciplines
Law
Literary Collections
Music
Poetry
Psychology
Science
…and many more.

Visit us at www.hardpress.net

Im TheStory
personalised classic books

JANE
IN
WONDERLAND

LEWIS
CARROLL

"Beautiful gift.. lovely finish.
My Niece loves it, so precious!"

Helen R Brumfieldon

⭐⭐⭐⭐⭐

UNIQUE GIFT

FOR KIDS, PARTNERS
AND FRIENDS

Timeless books such as:

Kids

Alice in Wonderland • The Jungle Book • The Wonderful Wizard of Oz
Peter and Wendy • Robin Hood • The Prince and The Pauper
The Railway Children • Treasure Island • A Christmas Carol

Adults

Romeo and Juliet • Dracula

Highly Customizable

Change Books Title

Replace Characters Names with yours

Upload Photo for inside page

Add Inscriptions

Visit
Im TheStory .com
and order yours today!

Lightning Source UK Ltd.
Milton Keynes UK
UKHW021028140520
363214UK00010B/1677